The Larger View:
Unitarians and Wo

Vernon Marshall

The Lindsey Press
London

Published by The Lindsey Press
on behalf of the General Assembly of Unitarian and
Free Christian Churches,
Essex Hall, 1–6 Essex Street, London WC2R 3HY, UK

ISBN 978-0-85319-074-5

Typeset by Garth Stewart, Oxford

Printed and bound in the United Kingdom by
Lightning Source, Milton Keynes

Now new times demand new measures,
and new ways we must explore;
let each faith bring its own treasures
to enrich the common store.
Then no more will creeds divide us –
though we love our own the best –
for the larger view will guide us
as we join in common quest.

(John Storey, 1935–1997)

Contents

Preface

In this study I have examined the relationship of British Unitarians to the historic world religions and reflected on the changes within the Unitarian movement as a consequence of that relationship. The challenge to the British Unitarian movement is to decide where it now stands in terms of its theological position. Whether it can still consider itself as part of the historic Christian Church, or whether the movement is better served by declaring itself to be an independent religion: these are the questions that this book tries to answer.

In preparing this study, based on a thesis submitted in partial fulfilment for the degree of Doctor of Ministry for the University of Derby, I am deeply indebted to Professor Paul Weller and Rev. David Hart, who, as my university supervisors, have been extremely helpful and inspirational throughout the period of my research. Thanks are due also to Rev. Dr. David Doel, who has read and commented on my work with very constructive advice. I am also grateful to all those colleagues who have allowed me to share with them my ideas for this research.

1 Introduction

This study is concerned with the relationship between British Unitarians and the world's major religions. In it I examine the way in which British Unitarianism has allowed, or even actively encouraged, beliefs and practices from other religions to permeate its own affirmations and pastoral practice. The thesis will be tested that British Unitarianism, once an avowedly Christian denomination, though a distinctly liberal one, is now a 'universalistic' or pan-religionist movement. The term 'universalistic' here does not refer to the belief in universal salvation but to the affirmation that all religious belief systems are equally valid. In this book it refers to the conviction that British Unitarianism as a whole no longer adheres unambiguously to a liberal form of Christianity but instead has become a home for individuals who seek their inspiration from whatever religious tradition speaks to their current theological condition. I will consider the historical evolution of this position, the state of affairs in contemporary Britain, and the implications for the practice of British Unitarianism today.

Chapter 1 is an introductory essay, examining the grounds for the study, defining the terms used, and describing the methodology employed. Chapter 2 will examine the British Unitarian contribution to the academic study of world religions and ask whether this has had any effect upon the theological character of the movement. Chapter 3 will consider the role of British Unitarians in inter-religious dialogue, in both historical and contemporary settings. Chapter 4 will reflect on contemporary practices that exemplify Unitarians' absorption of world religions into modern religious practice. The final chapter will reflect on the relationship between British Unitarianism and Christianity, and test the thesis that British Unitarianism is now a universalistic faith.

In more specific detail this initial chapter deals, firstly, with what it was that instigated the study, including the personal experience that led to my interest in this field of research. I will relate my own theological development since beginning to explore my Unitarian theology and describe how my religious stance has shifted so acutely as to lead me to question to what extent a similar experience may have affected other Unitarians. Secondly, in order for the study to have any coherence, I will examine briefly the theological evolution within the British Unitarian movement. A working definition of British Unitarianism will be identified in order to determine the nature of its current relationship with the world's religions. Although the study is concerned with British Unitarianism, there are links with the theological developments in the Unitarian and Universalist traditions in the United States of America; I will examine these traditions where necessary, clarifying where they relate to the British position. Thirdly, I will consider the research methods adopted for the study and justify their usage.

A personal journey

On joining a Unitarian congregation in 1977, I had little doubt in my own mind that British Unitarianism was a liberal Christian faith, although I acknowledge that there were individuals speaking for a minority of Unitarians who envisaged something akin to a federal world religion. 'This attitude, though often commended by Unitarians, probably does not reflect any very dominant trend in this country', commented the editors of a report on contemporary Unitarian faith (Kenworthy, 1964: 24). On seeking to understand something more about the history and theological position of the movement, I was given a number of books that would, it was believed, help to clarify matters for me. *Beliefs of a Unitarian* suggested that the British Unitarian movement was the 'religion of the larger affirmation', to the effect that 'instead of perceiving God incarnated in one man only, (Unitarians) ... reverence the divinity in all' (Hall, 1962: 7). Nevertheless, the book went on to itemise particular elements of Unitarianism in terms that would be understood only by mainstream Christians. Thus, there were sections on 'revelation and inspiration', 'the leadership of Jesus', 'the resurrection of Jesus', 'incarnation', and 'salvation'. The details dealt with in those sections suggested a radical theology, but there was nonetheless a concern to define Unitarian religion by reference to events in the life of Jesus and theories about the person of Jesus.

A major publication presented to me as representative of modern British Unitarianism was *Concerning Jesus* (Wigmore-Beddoes, 1975), a book offering six essays on current Unitarian Christology. Each essay acknowledged liberal Christianity as the norm. One significant essay within the book, 'Christianity and the Encounter of World Religions', made the claim that a study of the teachings of the world's religions was extremely valuable but that this did not mean relinquishing the need to spread knowledge of the life and teachings of Jesus (Midgley, 1975: 103). The essay also made clear that liberal Christians need not fear the practice of all-faith services 'so long as the pitfalls of eclecticism and syncretism are avoided' (*ibid.*: 107). The essay was written, it is significant to note, by someone who is now unlikely to express the views that he did in 1975.

My own theological position on entry to the Unitarian movement was, like my position on becoming a fully recognised minister in 1985, that of a liberal Christian keen to retain the Unitarian Christian heritage. This is made clear by the note to a prayer that I wrote for an anthology of Unitarian worship material in 1987 (Hughes, 1987: 31). Several years later I warned the Unitarian movement of the dangers of rejecting the liberal Christian heritage:

> *Alas, there are Unitarians today who would wish us to be purged of our past, who want us to be freed from our associations with liberal Christianity. What history does teach us is that those who ignore their own pasts are those whose future is in grave doubt. Where today are the Muggletonians, the Irvingites and the Theistic Churches?* (Marshall, 1990: 3)

Things began to change, however. A few years later, although I still considered myself a liberal Christian, I did feel a need to identify more with Unitarianism, even where it was not so clearly Christian, than I did with Christians who were not Unitarians. In a series of meetings over two years with other Unitarian ministers and lay leaders within the Midland Union district where I was at that time living and working, I discovered that my Christian position was not as strong as it had formerly been. This discovery was examined in an essay written for the professional journal of the Unitarian ministry.

> *Though still loyal to the Christian tradition, I cannot conceive of describing myself as a Christian without the Unitarian adjective. I can, however, be happy with the Unitarian label without the need for further definition.*
> (Marshall, 1992: 30)

My spiritual journey developed further towards a more mystical and nature-orientated theology. The firmness of my Christian convictions had evaporated somewhat with the embracing of feminist theology and the use of new and experimental metaphors for the divine. 'Look lovingly upon the world of nature and find therein evidence of that inexpressible something which defies definition' (Marshall, 1995: 14). This was followed by the composition of a number of collects employing the names of God used by all the world's great religions (Marshall, 1996: 5-8).

The full extent of my own theological transformation is apparent in an article that I wrote for the *New Age Unitarian Networkers' File*. I had clearly moved from a liberal Christianity to a nature-centred spirituality:

> *My earth-centred spirituality became crystallised when I came into contact with Druidry. Here was presented an integrated system that was focused on a calendar based on the natural cycles.* (Marshall, 1998: unpaginated)

What was it that encouraged me to shift my spiritual focus away from the liberal Christian tradition to something more eclectic? A number of factors may be considered as particularly relevant. Firstly, my position as Minister to the Unitarian New Meeting Church in Birmingham from 1985 until 1996 involved an unusually intensive involvement in inter-religious activity. Because of inner-city communal conflict within Birmingham, manifesting itself particularly in the riots in 1981 and 1985, I sought to be part of the process of inter-religious understanding and co-operation. This involved membership of the Birmingham Inter-Faith Council, the Birmingham Fellowship of Faiths, and, for slightly different reasons, the Birmingham Council of Christians and Jews. I also became an active member of the British Chapter of the International Association of Religious Freedom and took part in its local conferences. Throughout this period I became more aware of religious positions of which I had hitherto had only a basic knowledge.

A second relevant factor was the pursuing of research that led to a Master of Philosophy degree awarded by the Open University (2001). This examined the work in the field of Comparative Religion of the Unitarian minister and academic, Joseph Estlin Carpenter (1844–1927). As will be seen, Carpenter's own position became more liberal as he studied the philosophies of the religions of the East, especially those of Theravada and Pure Land Buddhism. In order for me to appreciate the work that

Carpenter did, it was necessary to have more than a mere grounding in the basic religious systems of those traditions studied by him.

Thirdly, British Unitarianism was shifting its theological focus. This development will be examined throughout this book. Although it is difficult to identify which aspects of this trend away from liberal Christianity influenced me, and why this happened, it is important to note that the British Unitarian movement has gone through a period of rapid change over the past thirty years. Either I changed because of the influence of the shifting religious environment, or the British Unitarian movement was itself changing to reflect the evolving perceptions of its constituency and the shifting social context. It is important now to consider the character of British Unitarianism at the time of my initial involvement, and how the movement had changed over the last two hundred years.

A definition of British Unitarianism

Reflection on the relationship between British Unitarianism and the world's religions requires the establishment of a working definition of British Unitarianism as it is today. Before doing this, however, it is essential to accept that British Unitarianism is an evolving movement whose theology has been in constant flux during the two centuries leading up to the present time.

The nineteenth century

Although Unitarianism was not the creation of the nineteenth century, that was the era in which the movement was at its most active and creative. It was in that century that the movement was formalised into a denominational structure with the creation, in 1825, of the British and Foreign Unitarian Association (BFUA) and, in 1882, of the National Conference of Unitarian, Free Christian, Liberal Christian, and Other Non-Subscribing and Kindred Congregations. According to a major history of the BFUA, British Unitarianism in that era was a Bible-based Christian denomination. 'Unitarian Christianity was...a Biblical Religion, accepting miracles, and rejecting creeds, not as incredible, but as non-Biblical' (Mellone, 1925: 67). The twenty-sixth Annual Report of the BFUA indicated that the Bible was the rule of faith of British Protestants and that '...it is the object of this Society to give strength and influence to that principle' (BFUA, 1851: 1).

5

Jesus was presented as a man like other men, who received the Holy Spirit at his baptism and was then endowed with supernatural capacities to carry out his work as the Messiah, revealing the reality of a future life where all would be rewarded according to their works (Belsham, 1811: 47). This Christology meant that Jesus was accorded a lesser status than that ascribed to him by mainstream Christianity, but it was one that focused, nevertheless, on Jesus as the ultimate revealer of God's wisdom. A major cause of anxiety to other Christians from mainstream denominations was that Unitarianism taught universal salvation, a doctrine that was powerfully impressed upon Unitarian thought by the most influential Unitarian layperson of his day, Thomas Southwood Smith (1788–1861) in his seminal work, *Illustrations of the Divine Government* (1816).

By the middle of the century, things began to change (Short, 1968: 254). The more conservative wing adhered unhesitatingly to traditional beliefs of doctrinal and Biblical Unitarianism. The more liberal wing instead emphasised tolerance and spiritual depth. The most significant British Unitarian thinker at this time, indeed of the whole nineteenth century, was James Martineau (1805–1900). In his *The Rationale of Religious Enquiry*, Martineau wrote that reason was superior to all else, and that even the Hebrew and Christian Scriptures were to be subject to it.

> *The question is intricate; but I will endeavour to make it clear, that no apparent inspiration whatever can establish any thing contrary to reason; that reason is the ultimate appeal, the supreme tribunal, to the test of which even scripture must be brought.* (Martineau, 1853: 62)

Martineau's approach did not go unchallenged, as is witnessed by the unsuccessful, but strongly supported, attempts to write a dependence on traditional scriptural bases into the constitution of the BFUA (Gordon, 1970: 49). Martineau justified his position by claiming that it was not a break with the past but a reinterpretation of orthodox teaching, a re-affirmation of the essence of Christianity. Traditional doctrines were denied, not because of their unscriptural foundation, but because even the writers of the Christian scriptures were subjected to the test of reason and conscience.

Martineau built on his ideas with his *A Study of Religion* (1900), seeking to create a religious system based on reason and conscience without drawing directly on the Hebrew and Christian scriptures. It was free philosophical thinking, resulting in a belief in a personal God, in a divine demand for ethical living, and a belief in the immortality of the soul. Martineau believed that religion and conscience produced what the historic creeds sought to express. For him there were underlying truths that were hidden by dogmatic concepts such as original sin and expiatory redemption, and myths like the Incarnation and the Second Coming. 'All are the growth of a mythical literature, or Messianic dreams, or Pharisaic theology, or sacramental superstition, or popular apotheosis' (1890: 650).

Throughout his life, Martineau asserted that, although his theology was radical, he was nonetheless a Christian, devoted to the life and person of Jesus Christ. It seems, however, that his liberation of Unitarianism from a Bible-based focus meant that British Unitarians could now move in different directions entirely. Francis Newman (1805–1897), for example, brother of the famous Cardinal, became a Unitarian only when he felt that his denial of the revealed character of the Christian Scriptures and the necessity of a mediator were sentiments welcomed in Unitarianism. The inspiration for his joining was a confession of faith written for use in the Clerkenwell Unitarian Church. This document was included in an appendix to the written version of a sermon explaining the reasons for Newman's admission into the Unitarian fold.

> *Faith in an infinitely perfect God is all our Theology. The Universe is our Divine Revelation. The Manifestations of Nature and the Devotional Literature of all Times and Peoples are our Bible. The goodness incarnated in humanity is our Christ. Every guide and helper is our Saviour. Increasing personal holiness is our salvation. The normal wonders of Nature are our Miracles. Love to God and love to man – piety and morality – are our only sacraments.* (Dean, 1875: 1)

Other Unitarians professed an idealistic pantheism inspired by Herbert Spencer (1820–1904). They saw in God a mysterious power working for the realisation of order and justice. Others saw the object of religion as the realisation of the human ideal, this ideal being divinised in order to render it available for reverence and worship. It has to be said, however, that such ideas represented only a minority of Unitarian opinion. Some argued that Christianity was being renewed by Unitarian radicalism. For many, Jesus was no longer a divine mediator but an extraordinary example of what human behaviour could be like. This was the view of a prominent preacher of the day, Richard Acland Armstrong (1843–1905). 'The Christ...we can take this man for our type and model of the loveliest and noblest humanity has ever been; and we can love him with all our heart and soul' (1881: 3).

The British Unitarian movement had reached a point of rapid theological change. Experimentation and theological challenge became customary. Theological speculations were considered as individual credos rather than as affirmations owned by the denomination as a whole. There were no longer any certainties. The philosophical basis for the movement was in great flux, and the tendency to explore and experiment was implicit. Such was the position at the end of the nineteenth century with the death of Martineau in 1900.

The twentieth century

By the beginning of the twentieth century, British Unitarianism was distancing itself from mainstream Christianity on the one hand and acknowledging the validity of the major religions of the world on the other. The identification of Unitarianism with Christianity had become cultural rather than doctrinal. This was significant, as Britain was slowly becoming a more diverse society in religious terms. If Unitarianism was identifying itself as Christian primarily because of its geographical location, then, should the national cultural character change, there would be less justification for retaining a Christian identity.

> *We live in an atmosphere and under a civilization whose best characteristics are steeped in the influence of Jesus. We are enlisted by birth, environment, and choice, under his banner.* (Flower, 1922: 104)

Slowly but surely Unitarianism in Britain was moving towards a position whereby all religions were being recognised as equally valid and acknowledged as different cultural expressions of the same reality. 'The prophets of God are many, but God is One' (*ibid.*: 105). An important publication, based on a survey of Unitarian theological concepts within British congregations and carried out by a national commission, established the need of the religions to share insights. Indian monism, for example, 'can be fully harmonized with what is essential in Christianity' (Holt, 1945: 143). A deepening of the contacts with other religions would, it was stated, lead to spiritual unity and 'a true and enduring world-society' (*ibid.*).

Unitarianism was now affirming more strongly that religion could be characterised by principles rather than by beliefs. Unitarians were upholding the virtues of human character, religious and civil liberty, tolerance towards those with different religious and political positions, and social reform. There was little attempt to define Unitarianism theologically, because individualism allowed for greatly differing doctrinal positions. That the beliefs of other religions were being taken seriously by Unitarians is evidenced by the warning given in the Minns Lecture delivered in 1959 by a prominent British minister who was soon to become the General Secretary of the Unitarian General Assembly: 'We must be aware of attempts at devising a synthetic religion made up of elements from all the great faiths' (Kielty, 1959: 46).

The Unitarian theological position was to some extent clarified with the work of a major enterprise begun in 1963. The Unitarian General Assembly established a commission to examine the theological views of its constituent congregations and adherents. Its findings were duly published the following year, when it identified six types of contemporary British Unitarianism (Kenworthy, 1964: 23-5). The largest group identified were the adherents of **'Liberal Protestant Christianity'**, a group that believed in 'essential Christianity', purged of its extreme supernatural elements and recognising Jesus as in no sense God but a source of insight and inspiration. The second group was also vaguely Christian, espousing **'Existential Unitarianism'**. These Unitarians acknowledged the interpretation of Christianity as myth, believing in the symbolic significance of much traditional dogma, particularly that relating to Jesus, when considered against the background of the human situation in a world of mystery, suffering, and death. The third type of contemporary Unitarianism, **'Non-Christocentric Theism'**, was based on belief in a personal God, or Universal Spirit, but with less emphasis on the centrality of Jesus than the first type. The fourth type, **'Universalism'**, affirmed the profound significance of all religious dispensations, with some sort of federation of all existing world religions as the ultimate goal. The fifth type, **'Religious Humanism'**, reflected a sort of religious agnosticism, doubting the value of the concept of a personal God and acknowledging humanity as the location of ultimate value. The sixth and final type defined was **'Unitarian Pragmatism'**. Unitarians of this kind were sceptical about metaphysical notions and any attempts to explain away the universe.

Religion was thought of in pragmatic terms as something that seemed to work, especially in the crises of birth, mating, and death.

The groups who identified with these six types of Unitarianism were not necessarily mutually exclusive, nor were they exhaustive. What the research recognised, however, was that British Unitarianism had become, theologically, very diverse. Between the period when the commission was undertaking its research and the end of the century, further rapid changes were taking place. The 1980s saw the birth of a new organisation within British Unitarianism, the Unitarian Renewal Group, a group of individuals who sought to bring the movement together on principles that celebrated theological diversity. It stressed the need to affirm the word *Unitarian* as a noun, with the various other appellations being appended merely as adjectives. Thus one could be a Christian Unitarian or a Humanist Unitarian and so on. This was a complete reversal of the usual practice whereby traditional adherents would define themselves as Unitarian Christians, in the belief that they were members of the historic Christian Church, of which the Unitarian denomination was only one of many components.

In 1985 another organisation was created within British Unitarianism, although its membership is not restricted to it. The Meditational Fellowship was formed to promote meditation as an individual and group practice, and to provide learning about theoretical aspects of meditation. It has produced material, for example, not only on the meditation traditions of Christianity, but on Vipassana Meditation (Monk, 1997), the Buddhist concept of *shunyata*, or emptiness (Monk, 1999), and the Buddhist practice of *karuna,* or compassion (Monk, 2001). This growing organisation aptly reflects the developing interest that British Unitarianism has acquired in the philosophical and practical aspects of other religions.

In the 1990s emerged an even more radical group within the Unitarian movement in Britain. Initially known as the Unitarian Neo-Pagan Network, it later promoted itself as the New Age Unitarian Network and created within itself a home for those Unitarians who were inspired by various trends that had migrated from the West Coast of the United States. It thus explored philosophies such as monism, the human potential movement, and cosmic evolutionary optimism. Within a few years, however, it had become more clearly identifiable as an organisation for Unitarian Neo-Pagans. Having changed its name in 2000 to the

Unitarian Earth Spirit Network, it promoted its objects, as indicated on the cover of its *Network File*, as 'revering the totality of the divine reality being revealed to us through the infinite multiplicity of forms and forces', and, more importantly, 'affirming a Pagan spiritual perspective as being fully compatible with the human quest for self-knowledge and ultimate meaning' (Mitchell, 2000: back cover).

The fact that some Unitarians had begun to feel that the liberal Christian position was under threat is evidenced by the creation in 1991 of another organisation, the Unitarian Christian Association. In a sense its creation was an acknowledgement that to equate British Unitarianism with liberal Christianity was now a thing of the past.

Thus, as can be seen, the British Unitarian movement had, by the end of the twentieth century, become a movement with an enormously broad spectrum of belief. The changes that had begun in the early Victorian period had now progressed to an extreme position of liberality and tolerance. At this point in history, however, the formal position of the British Unitarian General Assembly had failed to keep in tune with the theological developments taking place within its constituent congregations and individual membership. Nevertheless, within a few years, and with the dawning of a new century, the General Assembly had rewritten its aims and objects to acknowledge this evolutionary change.

The twenty-first century

In April 2001 the British Unitarian General Assembly revised its Objects in order to represent the views of its members more accurately. Although the former Objects merely sought 'to promote pure Religion in the Worship of God and the Service of Man', they also called for 'the diffusion and support of the principles of Unitarian Christianity' (GA, 2000:7). The new Objects treated Unitarian Christianity in a very different way. Their commitment to Christianity was much less emphatic.

> *The Object of the Assembly is: to promote a free and inquiring religion through the worship of God and the celebration of life; the service of humanity and respect for all creation; and the* upholding *of the liberal Christian tradition.* (my emphasis) (GA, 2001: 7)

There was also a commitment to 'learn from the spiritual, cultural and intellectual insights of all humanity' (GA, 2001: 7). The language had also changed to reflect current concern to avoid sexist terminology. What was particularly remarkable about the process that led to the rewriting of this Object was the easy manner in which it was accepted by the movement. Some years earlier a similar change had been suggested; following a long exercise of consultation, it was not accepted by a sufficiently large percentage of the membership for it to become an integral part of the Constitution of the General Assembly. This time, however, the proponents of change encountered much less opposition.

In conclusion, in order to understand what effect the world's great religions have had upon British Unitarianism, it is necessary to appreciate the enormous changes that have taken place in the past two hundred years, and especially the remarkably rapid developments in recent years. This book will explore the role that the world's religions have played in these developments, together with the practical differences that have occurred as a result of such changes. In order to reflect on these changes, it is thus necessary to put in place a working definition of British Unitarianism. In the light of the foregoing historical review of British Unitarian theology, it should be sufficient to assert that modern Unitarianism in Britain is a movement that is based on principles, rather than on theology. It acknowledges its origins in liberal Christianity, and respects them, but now affirms the right of its individual members to find their own religious position. One Unitarian publication, still used as a textbook for those studying modern Unitarianism, and a source for religious exploration in congregational Religious Education exercises, sums up the British Unitarian position as it is today.

> *The Unitarian path is a liberal religious movement rooted in the Jewish and Christian traditions but open to insights from world faiths, reason and science; and with a spectrum extending from liberal Christianity through to religious humanism.* (Hill, 1994: 5)

Some considerations of method

The aim of this book is to identify the process that has led to a significant change in the theology and practice of British Unitarianism brought about by its relationship with other religions. This aim was pursued principally by a literature review and a questionnaire. There were also minor discussions and consultations, but these were of an informal nature. My research methods will now be considered in turn.

The literature review

A literature review was felt to be appropriate, as Unitarian literature on world religions appeared to have a different character from parallel studies pursued by scholars from other traditions. Unitarians were critical of scholars who studied world religions in order to refute what they taught. One prominent scholar, for example, berated Sir Monier Monier-Williams (1819–1899), the celebrated Indologist, for referring to Hinduism, Buddhism, and Islam as 'the chief false religions' (J.E. Carpenter, 1900: 7). The early Unitarian scholars, however, sought to extend their knowledge of other faiths in order to deepen their own. Initially, there was no desire for inter-religious dialogue, but a wish to discover how strong their own position was when compared with the tenets of other religions. This is the position, or 'model' (Cohen and Manion, 1994: 16), that is adopted in this study. Its usage helps in the understanding of how British Unitarians were to approach the study of world religions.

Unitarians did not study other religions in order to refute them, but they did have a specific aim nonetheless. Carpenter, for example, believed that by exploring the faith of others the centrality of the message of Jesus and the belief in monotheism would be assured. He acknowledged the nobility of the Eastern religions, but nevertheless accorded a higher place to Jesus.

> *We must conceive the religions of the world as all in turn contributing with varied potencies. Foremost among them, at least in this stage of our development, is the Christianity we love.* (1911: 113)

A literature review was thus considered a necessary means of identifying something distinctive within the movement's published material. I therefore sought to read all the movement's publications dealing with the relationship of British Unitarianism with other religions, and with internal theological development. Although an enormous task, it was felt to be the only way of gaining sufficient insight that a study such as this demands.

There were difficulties with such an approach, however. Firstly, in some fields there has been a paucity of material. There is little material, for example, concerning earlier attempts by British Unitarians to study world religions or to engage in dialogue with their adherents – Sir William Jones (1746–1794) being a notable exception. The relationships between British Unitarianism and Judaism have also gone largely unrecorded, despite the pioneering work of Robert Travers Herford (1860–1950). Publications in the later period, particularly from the middle of the twentieth century, have been mostly minor projects, and I have had to rely a good deal on publications with a smaller readership than the works published in the late Victorian period by American Unitarians such as James Freeman Clarke (1810–1888) and Ralph Waldo Emerson (1803–1882). As such smaller publications tend to be read mostly by Unitarians, it has been difficult to assess how modern Unitarian approaches to world religions have been viewed by those outside the movement. Work produced for internal consumption does not always have the same character and objectivity as a work seeking to satisfy a larger, and often more critical, readership.

Secondly, because much of the later material comprised ideas that were published without an objective refereeing process, it has been difficult to determine how far such ideas reflected a general trend in theological development, and how far their authors were prepared to defend their positions. On the other hand, such material is instant, it reflects the sudden mood changes of those pursuing a particular theological line, and it thus provides a snapshot picture of an issue of the time. If such material is to be considered as authoritative, then it can be so only if supported by other research approaches, such as those also pursued.

The questionnaire

The questionnaire was designed to elicit information and ideas based on three major themes. First, I sought to discover the extent of the involvement of Unitarians in inter-religious dialogue. Second, I wished to determine how far other religions had influenced the British Unitarian movement in terms of religious and philosophical ideas, the use of sacred literature, and the observance of sacred calendars. Third, by reference to the data, I have reflected on how inter-religious dialogue has affected the character of British Unitarianism.

The questionnaire was sent to Unitarian ministers and accredited lay leaders. Every minister, lay pastor, and lay leader on the Rolls of the General Assembly was sent a questionnaire – with some exceptions. Ministers and lay leaders were chosen as recipients on the grounds that, with their theological training, and with regular exploration of theological ideas through the conduct of worship and religious education programmes, they were likely to be able to answer most authoritatively. Ministers of the Non-Subscribing Church of Ireland were not included, on the grounds that there is within it a different culture, basis of faith, and form of governance that, although an affiliate of the General Assembly, sets it apart as a separately constituted denomination. To include ministers of the NSPCI could have seriously affected interpretation of the data. Also excluded were ministers living abroad who had had little or no contact with the British movement for some time, and a number of retired ministers who were too frail to participate in the exercise.

Ultimately, one hundred questionnaires were sent out by post or email, and eighty were eventually returned. The names of those who returned the questionnaires are listed in Appendix 1; they include ministers and lay leaders from many different theological persuasions and from a range of geographical localities. Both sexes were well represented, and there were responses from full-time ministers, those with part-time appointments, and retirees. Follow-up letters were sent to those who did not initially respond, and every encouragement was given to complete the questionnaires, despite reluctance on the part of some. Quite a number were returned after some pressure from me, as I was determined not to have distorted results, on the grounds that, as has been asserted by some researchers, people who do not return questionnaires are different from those who do (Moser and Kalton, 1971: 267-8). Several colleagues in the local area piloted the questionnaire, all of whom then declared that the process of completing it was neither a difficult nor lengthy exercise.

Where the questionnaire was particularly successful was in indicating, firstly, the extensive knowledge of, and association with, other religions and their adherents, and secondly, the vast theological diversity within the British Unitarian movement. No fewer than 27 different definitions were identified. This information was vital in enabling me to draw conclusions about the character and direction of British Unitarianism.

Other methods

In order to extend the range of views, informal consultations were made with Unitarians who do not share the notion that British Unitarianism is fundamentally a universalistic movement. There are Unitarians who feel that, although insights from world religions are of great value, the movement is still basically a liberal Christian denomination, the status of Jesus being enhanced by comparison with the leading figures of other religions. A declaration dating from 1982 still reflects the views of many: 'in essence and origin, we *are* a Christian group, affirming the uni-personality of God' (Long, 1982: 4), but '(Unitarian Christianity) gladly acknowledges the tremendous relevance and importance of the great non-Christian World Faiths' (*ibid.*: 10).

Similarly, approaches were made to the representatives of the several organisations within the British Unitarian movement that promote a particular position. Thus, reference is made in this study to the Unitarian Christian Association, an organisation that seeks to preserve traditional Unitarian Christianity, and discussions were held with its officers. The same approach was made to the Unitarian Renewal Group, a loosely organised group established to celebrate the concept of Unitarianism as an inclusive body, recognising Unitarian values as central, with different religious emphases being acknowledged as secondary. I also approached members of the Unitarian Earth Spirit Network, the body within British Unitarianism that welcomes insights from the Pagan tradition.

Conclusion

As can be seen, there is a need to balance the historical review with the practice of contemporary Unitarianism. There is, nevertheless, a need to view the position of modern Unitarianism in context, by reflecting on the stages in the historical development of the movement. This is where the study properly begins, and the following chapter examines the work of those Unitarians who first encountered other religions as objects of academic study.

2 The academic study of religions

Introduction

The first chapter set the scene for the book as a whole. It explained why I wished to engage in such a study, and what the research involved. This second chapter examines the ways in which British Unitarianism has undertaken the academic study of other religions. It seeks to identify the phases of development in British Unitarians' approach to the comparative study of religions. The first phase, which I have called 'the Tentative Phase', considers the work of Unitarians who pioneered the study of other religions but whose findings had no visible impact upon the theology or practice of British Unitarianism. The second phase I have called 'the Comparative Phase', alluding to the exercise of drawing parallels between the Unitarian Christianity of the day and the theologies of the other world religions under scrutiny. I have called the third phase 'the Integral Phase', to define the modern position of British Unitarians wherein engagement with the ideas, theologies, and philosophies of other religions is considered integral to the Unitarian tradition.

It is important to note here that my use of the term 'Comparative Religion' is now problematic. I continue to use the term, as it was an expression used in earlier times to reflect the notion that Christianity was the norm against which all other religions were to be compared. It is a term that is in less common use today, when colleges and universities seek to deal with the world's religions with equal consideration. 'The History of Religion' and 'The Study of Religions', or, in continental Europe, 'the Scientific Study of Religion', are terms that are now thought to be more in keeping with that approach.

The Tentative Phase

The 'Tentative Phase' in the development of British Unitarians' academic study of other religions covers the period from 1786, when Sir William Jones published his first work, until the appearance of Estlin Carpenter's comparative studies in the 1870s. During this period there was an attempt to uncover the ideas behind other religions, but it was only a minor enterprise, conducted by a few Unitarians. There was no suggestion that such ideas could have an impact upon Unitarian faith. It is important to note here, however, that this was generally the case with the study of Comparative Religion.

Comparative Religion in the Tentative Phase

The eighteenth and early nineteenth centuries were a period for the publication of numerous books about newly discovered religions. It was a time when books about religions were meant to inform, without any detailed analysis of the religion in question and without the need to compare or contrast it with Christianity. The signal exception in this regard was the study of Chinese religion. Scholars who were influenced by Gottfried Wilhelm Leibniz (1646–1716), and others who would prepare the ground for, and be active in, the period in Western intellectual history known as 'the Enlightenment', emphasised individual freedom of intellectual enquiry and personal commitment to reason. Believing Chinese religion to be free of doctrines of revelation, the Deists in particular looked upon it as their model, in the belief that China had actually lived 'natural religion'. 'Mosaic and Chinese chronologies were compared, not always to the former's advantage' (Sharpe, 1975: 17). Christian Wolff (1679–1754), Johann Wolfgang von Goethe (1749–1832), and Voltaire (1694–1778) were all admirers of Chinese religion and wisdom (*ibid.*).

Apart from this preoccupation with China, scholars produced an increasing stream of books dealing with the religions of the world. There was little attempt, however, to place religions in their cultural contexts or to compare them favourably with Christianity. Such works were compendia of religions, detailing the ceremonies and lifestyles of primal communities (*ibid.*: 18). There was very little sympathy expressed for believers of other religions or their practices: words such as 'fetishism' were used to describe the basis of these other 'cults', the word 'fetishism' being introduced in a book by the scholar Charles de Brosse (1709–1777), published in 1760: *Du Cultes des Dieux Fétiches* (reprinted 1972). A few years earlier, the Scottish philosopher, David Hume (1711–1776), had criticised polytheism as being 'the playsome whimsies of monkies in human shape' (1757, reprinted 1957: 65). This particularly insensitive approach to the study of other religions is important to remember when the Unitarian approach to Comparative Religion is considered, and especially when the beginnings of research into other religions by Unitarians is examined.

It was during this Tentative Phase that Unitarianism itself was becoming identifiable as an organised religious movement. The first congregation to adopt the name 'Unitarian' was founded in 1774 by Theophilus Lindsey (1723–1808). A number of English Presbyterian ministers and congregations were moving towards a non-Trinitarian position at this time, however, in the tradition of John Biddle (1615–1662) and others who had become sceptical of traditional creeds but had yet to formulate a coherent doctrinal position (Gow, 1928: 28-9). Lindsey's initiative accelerated the process of acknowledging a clearly stated free Christianity, which led to the establishment of a denominational structure in 1825 with the creation of the British and Foreign Unitarian Association (Mellone, 1925: 29-48). Until its creation, there were nevertheless a number of individuals, such as Joseph Priestley (1733–1804), who considered themselves 'Unitarian' in that they believed in 'the simple humanity of Jesus' (Mellone, 1925: 86).

Sir William Jones (1746–1794)

One of the first Europeans to discover the sacred literature of India was a Unitarian of the kind defined above. William Jones, 'one of the greatest polymaths in history' (Murray, 1999: frontispiece), was a distinguished scholar who became a Fellow of the Royal Society before he was forty years of age. A judge in the Supreme Court of Bengal, he was later to become a parliamentarian and political reformer (Holt, 1938: 75). While still a student at Oxford, he studied Persian and took extra lessons in Arabic from a native of Aleppo. In his twenties he had produced seven major works on those two languages.

While working in Bengal, Jones studied Sanskrit grammar and Hindu law, and published the *Asiatic Researches*, the first European journal devoted to Oriental studies. In 1786 he compared the languages of Sanskrit, Latin, and Greek and concluded that they had similar grammars. It was his belief that their similarities were not accidental (Lowenstein, 1996: 150) and that there was thus a historical relationship between South

European and Indian culture. Jones then went on to translate, in 1789, the classical Sanskrit play *Shakuntala*, believed to have been written by Kalidasa in the fifth century. This work has been claimed as an inspiration for the writing of the Prologue to Goethe's *Faust* and one of the poems of Percy Bysshe Shelley (1792–1822) (Robinson, 1999: 21). Jones then translated the Hindu laws of Manu in 1794. He planned a complete digest of Hindu and Muslim laws, but died before his project was completed.

As far as the Unitarian discovery of other religions is concerned, Jones' work is significant. There is no evidence of Unitarians before him having made any attempt to study other religions. That is perhaps not surprising, as Unitarianism had not yet become an organised movement. Nevertheless, Jones, as a Unitarian, was a pioneer and laid the ground for later explorations in the field of Comparative Religion.

Another unique aspect of Jones' contribution is the fact that he actually related to Hindus on a personal level, living close to Indian people. In the next century, as will be seen, Unitarian scholars were to write detailed analyses of Indian religion without actually visiting India or Indian communities elsewhere. Connected with this, however, is a feature of his work that was paralleled by later Unitarian scholars. Jones was solely concerned with written documents, rather than with the practice of Hinduism. He was not a scholar of religious studies as such, and did not display an interest in Hinduism from a phenomenological position.

There are positive features of Jones' work that elevate him to a position of some significance for British Unitarianism and its relationship with other religions. He connected the languages of Sanskrit with Latin and Greek, and, although he was not the first to suggest a philological link, he was the first to put the idea on a sound footing. He has thus been considered the founder of comparative philology, also known as historical linguistics (Robinson, 1999: 21). Jones' example also suggested that Indian literature in itself was worthy of study. This was a sharp contrast to those in the eighteenth century who considered non-European races as unlikely to produce anything worthy.

William Adam (1796–1881)

Few British Unitarians took an interest in other religions during the Tentative Phase. A second exception was the Scotsman, William Adam, who was originally a Baptist missionary in Serampore, India and whose work has often been overlooked (Hill, 1995: 39). After mastering the classical Sanskrit and Bengali languages, he joined a group of scholars revising the Bengali translation of the Christian Scriptures. What he produced, however, was a compilation of the ethical sayings of Jesus from the synoptic gospels, and the project was criticised for misrepresenting Christianity (Medhurst, 1992: 5-6).

One of Adam's colleagues was Rammohun Roy (1772–1883), the scholarly Hindu. Roy was a Hindu thinker who became familiar with Western ideas through his work with the East India Company. He was influenced by Western rational theism and had relationships with English Unitarians, particularly through his correspondence with Lant Carpenter (1780–1840). He sailed to England in 1830 as envoy of the Mogul Emperor but died in Bristol in 1833 while visiting the Carpenter family. Roy upheld his belief in Advaita Vedanta, but interpreted its teachings in a rationalistic way, identifying knowledge of Brahman with the rational contemplation of God as revealed in nature. Adam tried to convert Roy to Trinitarianism but was instead convinced by Roy to adopt the opposite view (Sen, 1967: 3). Adam subsequently resigned his position and, along with a number of Indians and Europeans, formed the Calcutta Unitarian Society. This society lasted seven years until its Hindu members created a new body, based on a Unitarian form of Hinduism, the Brahmo Samaj, a movement that, though theistic, rejected the type of theism characteristic of Christianity (Sastri, 1907: 261) and thus left Unitarian Christianity behind. Influenced by Islam, Christianity, and modern science, it sought a return to what it considered to be the purity of Hindu ideals, by rejecting the use of images in worship and by reforming Hindu social practices.

Adam, 'a man of great learning and singularly varied experience' (Carter, 1902: 2), played an important role in the tentative discovery of non-Christian religions for two reasons. First, his linguistic skills were employed in such a manner that Hindu theological concepts influenced how he thought about Christian doctrines. He did not merely take note of what Hinduism affirmed, but adjusted his own faith in the light of the linguistic expression of what to him were foreign concepts. Secondly, his part in the creation of the Brahmo Samaj must not be underrated. Without his initiative and drive, the Brahmo Samaj might never have been created. Its leaders developed a school of thought that found its full expression in the so-called 'Bengal Renaissance'. Later scholars viewed the Samaj's position as representing an original Hindu monotheism that had been obscured by the later embellishments of image-worship and elaborate ritual (J.E. Carpenter, 1912). Adam thus had a very significant part to play in bringing the religious ideas of India to the attention of British Unitarians. The Tentative Phase, owing to Adam, thus quickly opened the way for a new approach to the world's religions, one that was more challenging and was more likely to impinge on personal faith.

The Comparative Phase

The second phase in the history of British Unitarianism's academic study of other religions coincided approximately with the period that began with the appearance of Estlin Carpenter's works in the 1870s and ended soon after his death in 1927. At a time of general and growing interest in Comparative Religion, Unitarians were now beginning to look at other religions with a critical eye, comparing their beliefs with those of their own Unitarian Christianity. A number of Unitarian scholars were making reputations for themselves in this important field. It is necessary, however, firstly to reflect on the general character of the Comparative Religion scene during this period.

Comparative Religion 1870–1930

Comparative Religion was not a new field of enquiry during this period. Nevertheless, it came to the attention of the wider public in the 1860s and 1870s (Sharpe, 1975: 1). The year 1859 saw the publication of a book that was to have a tremendous impact upon Victorian minds: Charles Darwin's *On the Origin of Species by Means of Natural Selection.* Thus began a renewed search for human origins, and the evolutionary theory expounded by scholars such as Jean-Baptiste Lamarck (1744–1829), James Hutton (1726–1797), Charles Lyell (1797–1875) and Charles Darwin (1809–1882) was applied with some vigour to religion.

Although Darwin wrote from a scientific perspective, the influence of the evolutionary theory was widespread. Those taking an interest in other religions embraced it, although by doing so they appeared to identify more closely with science than with religion in the dispute between the two. Christianity had depended on the notion that humankind was the ultimate and supreme act of divine creation, and science seemed to undermine that position. To some, religion appeared to be redundant and unnecessary, and Christianity had to struggle to retain its position of dominance. With some exceptions, organised Christianity regarded other religions as beyond salvation. Now there was a growing interest in examining other religions as part of the project of discovering the phases of human development.

For those expounding the theory of evolution, the plurality of religious expression was a conundrum, and it was believed that only scientific methods could find a solution to it. The principle adopted was that of comparison. The term 'Comparative Religion' became more widely used as the practice of comparing religious beliefs, writings, and practices became more widespread.

Several approaches were used in order to apply this non-dogmatic principle. First, there was the **philological approach**. Pursued by Friedrich Max Müller (1823–1900), this approach took the view that reason and speech grew together, and that therefore there was a need to discover the roots of language (Müller, 1856). This would reveal religious concepts to demonstrate how far the community in question had made sense of its environment. Secondly, there was the **anthropological approach** pursued by scholars such as John Lubbock (1834–1913) in, for example, his book *Prehistoric Times* (1872); Edward Burnett Tylor (1832–1917), in, among other documents, *Primitive Culture* (1904); and Andrew Lang (1844–1912), author of *Modern Mythology* (1898). Evolutionary theory had allowed anthropology to investigate religion as a means of demonstrating the stages through which humankind had passed on the way to an advanced spiritual outlook. Thirdly, there was the approach based on the **psychology of religion**, pursued in the main by American scholars such as Granville Stanley Hall (1844–1924), James Leuba (1868–1946), and William James (1842–1910). Psychology in this period did not limit itself to consideration of human behaviour but was a wider field of study, dealing with all non-material aspects of the human mind. Fourthly, there was the **folklore approach**, pursued by Sir James Frazer (1854–1941), author of the seminal *The Golden Bough* (1922).

Comparative Religion was a discipline that sought to be scientific, and the evolutionary theory gave it additional vigour. It had yet, however, to determine a character for itself. It was in such an environment that Unitarian scholars worked and made their discoveries. The most notable of those scholars was Estlin Carpenter. Carpenter had a major contribution to make to Comparative Religion, but, as will be seen, the contribution of American Unitarians had an influence upon him also.

Joseph Estlin Carpenter (1844–1927) and his American forebears

Carpenter was a Unitarian minister and scholar who became Principal of Manchester College, Oxford and the first in that city to lecture on Comparative Religion, although initially he did so outside the auspices of the University. He was also a Biblical scholar, and, as Principal of the College, had major responsibility for the training of candidates for the Unitarian ministry. He is acknowledged by Unitarians as being of primary importance for his contribution to Comparative Religion (Long, 1986: 267). He produced no fewer than 37 articles, essays, and books on various aspects of Comparative Religion, or the beliefs of other religions, and was widely respected in his day for his extensive knowledge of the subject (Cross, 1957). His particular interest was Buddhism, and he became one of the leading Pali scholars of his day, although other religions engaged his interest too (Long, 1986: 281).

Carpenter acknowledged the influence of the American Unitarians of the Transcendentalist school, in particular William Rounseville Alger (1822–1905) and James Freeman Clarke (J.E. Carpenter, 1925: 16). Transcendentalism was a movement that challenged traditional Bible-based Unitarianism. Influenced by German philosophy and the new Biblical Criticism, it was inspired by, among others, Immanuel Kant (1724–1804) and Johann Gottfried Fichte (1762–1814). This radical school of thought, whose main champion was Ralph Waldo Emerson (1803–1882), called for a personal religion whereby individuals sought to discover the divine for themselves. It both questioned the miraculous foundations of Christianity on the one hand and found sympathy with the religions of the East on the other. It was a reaction against the Enlightenment rationalism of their day and offered 'a naturalist spirituality, a naturalist mysticism, without metaphysics and supernaturalism' (Higgins, 2003: 3).

Alger was a minister who began to take an interest in the religious writings of the East, as his study of Indian poetry indicates (1857). His greatest work was *A Critical History of the Doctrine of a Future Life*, originally published in 1860 and reissued in 1968. The book gave a detailed description of the major teachings of the world's religions, by placing the doctrines of Eastern religions alongside those of the Hebrew and Christian Scriptures, to show up similarities and differences. The major focus of the book was to draw attention to what Alger considered to be evidence of a universal religious experience. The result was to make the doctrines of other religions accessible, and this is what appealed to Carpenter. The book demonstrated that Christianity was not the only religion derived from a personal founder, or the sole possessor of sacred books containing important truths. 'With clear-eyed perception did one of the best loved Boston pastors grasp the significance of the new knowledge' (J.E. Carpenter, 1925: 16).

Carpenter paid tribute also (1925: 16) to Freeman Clarke, a minister and academic who eventually became Professor of Theology at Harvard University. Clarke's Unitarian and Transcendentalist notions led him to seek meaning in religious traditions other than his own. Over against the total condemnation of 'heathen' religions in the Christian tradition, the Transcendentalists discovered God's universal providence. 'It has become more usual of late to rehabilitate heathenism, and to place it on the same level as Christianity, if not above it' (Clarke, 1871: 14). In 1871, Clarke made his greatest contribution to Comparative Religion when Volume I of his two-volume *Ten Great Religions* was published. The book summarised the ten religions that he chose to study, separating out the 'ethnic' religions (i.e. Egyptian, Greek, Roman, Scandinavian, and Hindu faiths) from the 'catholic' religions (i.e. Judaism, Christianity, Islam, Buddhism, and Zoroastrianism). The book was genuinely comparative, in that the religions were compared in accordance with a number of topics such as God, the Soul, the Future Life, Prayer and Worship, and Salvation.

Inspired by these two American scholars, Carpenter affirmed that other religions had a role to play in his scheme of history. A convinced evolutionist, Carpenter recognised a oneness of purpose in all the religions. They were simply different manifestations of the same movement towards the unknown destiny determined by God. For Carpenter there was no dichotomy between true and false religion (Carpenter, 1893: 848). This approach was very radical, in that it seemed to suggest that all religions were of equal validity. This was a contrast to other Unitarians, who, although they acknowledged other religions as having value for human progress, nonetheless believed that only Christianity possessed the whole truth (Clarke, 1883: 373).

Carpenter saw no rivalry between the religions in their claims for teaching the truth because, for him, religious understanding was based on quite a different premise. God's plan for humankind was about a gradual unfolding of the divine purpose. This was received in different ways in different ages, and there was thus no split between truth and falsehood. There were simply different levels of awareness. The diverse religious scene was thus a theatre of order and progression.

Another major contribution made by Carpenter to the field of Comparative Religion was his role as a populariser. In his works he used simple expressions, designed to appeal to the non-specialist reader. *Comparative Religion* (1913) is typical of this. It had a wide circulation and went though five reprints, the last one more than 30 years after the original production. It was also a useful source book, the bibliography alone being a useful resource in indicating the scholarship available in 1913. Carpenter avoided technical language. In 'How Japanese Buddhism appeals to a Christian Theist' (1906), for example, he aimed for a simple rather than academic approach. This enabled him to reach a more general readership than would otherwise have been the case. Another example is *Theism in Medieval India* (1921). Although a monument of learning and religious insight, it was written in a lucid and attractive style and well within the searching mind of most students. Carpenter's works were popular because of their accessibility to a large number of people.

That Comparative Religion was Carpenter's major interest is evidenced by the fact that he retained appointments in teaching the subject when other interests had been renounced. In 1899, for example, he resigned as Vice-Principal and full Professor of Manchester College, but retained his position as Case Lecturer in Comparative Religion. This lectureship was sponsored by George Case (1824–1883), a former priest of both the Church of England and the Roman Catholic Church. The resources were to be administered by the Hibbert Trust as the trustees saw fit. Carpenter continued as Case Lecturer in Comparative Religion until 1924. After a period as Principal of the College from 1906 to 1915, he retired to take up an additional post, as Wilde Lecturer in Natural and Comparative Religion, this time with the University of Oxford.

Comparative Religion thus became an integral part of the curriculum of the College, students for the Unitarian ministry undertaking the study of it for each of their three years of training as a compulsory subject (Manchester College, 1915: 4). The other English college engaged in training students for the Unitarian ministry, The Unitarian College in Manchester, adopted Comparative Religion as an integral part of its curriculum in 1904, when the Faculty of Theology was established at the new Victoria University of Manchester. Students took their courses at the University under the lectureship of Professor T. W. Rhys Davids (1843–1922), although the subject was studied for only one year (McLachlan, 1915: 162). By the end of this phase, then, Comparative Religion was firmly rooted in Unitarian scholarship, although its acceptance was still not universal. In 1898, for example, Martineau had criticised Carpenter's resignation from Manchester College, the latter wishing to give himself more time to study Buddhism and the Pali language. Martineau called the resignation 'a retrogression from articulate to matriculate speech' (quoted by Deacon, 1977: 37).

The Integral Phase

This phase in the history of British Unitarianism's academic study of the world's religions covers the period from the death of Estlin Carpenter to the present. It is characterised by the insistence that such a discipline was and is integral to denominational principles. This study shows how Comparative Religion, or the History of Religions, has become a vital element in the culture of British Unitarianism. Inter-religious dialogue and the integration of the ideas of other religions into a Unitarian theological position are for consideration in later chapters. There have been profound consequences for the movement's treatment of other religions. To put the issue into context, however, there is once again a need to consider the development of Comparative Religion in the wider field.

Comparative Religion in modern times

It is an impossible task to encapsulate all the trends in modern Comparative Religion into a few paragraphs. This section aims to give only a very generalised indication of the state of such study at a time when British Unitarians were embracing it as an essential discipline for the training of its ministers and for those Unitarians who wished to explore more fully the factors influencing modern Unitarian thought.

The earliest notable factor in the twentieth century that influenced the direction of Comparative Religion was the decline in optimism generated by the massive loss of life in the Great War of 1914–1918. The idea of a steady evolution in human progress was now, inevitably, discredited. The time was thus ripe for new approaches to Comparative Religion, and these appeared from different directions. Bronislaw Malinowski (1884–1942) was a major figure associated with the approach that more or less discarded a consideration of history. Instead of theorising about the remote origins of religions, concentration was focused on the actual day-to-day lives of ordinary believing communities. Factors other than theology were brought into consideration when analysing religion, including, thanks to Max Weber (1864–1920), the economic background of a religious community (Ling, 1973: 43).

A contrary approach was less interested in social phenomena and more concerned with the individual experience. This approach was influenced by the psychologists who were interested in all aspects of the conscious mind. It was not interested in religion as a social phenomenon but was, nevertheless, as exemplified by Sigmund Freud (1856–1939), keen to pursue an accurate study of religious phenomena as components of mental pathology (Freud, 1962). There was some interest in history, but only in the form of mythology and its contribution to the way that religion is experienced as a present phenomenon. Carl Gustav Jung (1875–1961) was particularly influential in this direction and, in the search for a further understanding of the 'collective unconscious', made a study of Gnosticism and alchemy (Jung, 1963: 205).

Another approach that has had a long-lasting influence, and with which Gerardus van der Leeuw (1890–1950) was most associated, is the phenomenology of religion. This seeks to eliminate value judgments, to allow believers to speak for themselves, and to make an objective assessment of the role of religion in human life. It seeks to classify phenomena, to withdraw to one side in order to observe, to clarify and comprehend, and to testify to what is understood (van der Leeuw, reprinted 1948).

The major consequence of the various approaches in the twentieth century has been to discard Comparative Religion in its traditional form. There has been less emphasis on a comparative approach whereby certain religions are considered in parallel and their different doctrines analysed side by side, usually treating Christianity as the 'normative' religion alongside which others are compared. The name of an organisation formed in 1950, the International Association for the History of Religions, indicates this less exclusive approach. By the 1970s, university departments were changing their names and their courses, often adopting the title 'Religious Studies', or 'the Study of Religion(s)'. Where British Unitarianism has fitted into this evolution of ideas will now be considered, with particular reference to those Unitarians who contributed to this approach.

Will Hayes (1890–1959)

The name of Hayes is not widely known outside the Unitarian movement and, within British Unitarianism itself, his scholarly research in the field of other religions is not fully acknowledged. Not one of the ministers or lay leaders in the survey conducted as part of my research quoted Hayes as a source for the changing theological position of British Unitarianism. It is perhaps ironic that his material is known and used more by the Pagan movement than by Unitarians (Robertson, 2003: 6-7; Westwood, 1998: 7).

Hayes was a British Unitarian minister who served for most of his career at the Unitarian Church in Chatham, Kent. While there he set up an organisation called the Order of the Great Companions, identifying all the great religious leaders of the world's different traditions as equally valid. He wrote a great deal, organised conferences, and became something of a champion for the cause of universalism or 'pan-religionism'.

No systematic research on Hayes' work has ever been carried out, although a brief history of his contribution to Comparative Religion appears in my chapter in a modern book on Unitarian thought (Marshall, 1999). Nor has there been any clear explanation for the failure of his work to survive into the present. Nevertheless, there are indicators to suggest why his approach was considered somewhat controversial in its time. Firstly, his theological position – that there was only one genuine religion, the religion of the world – never attracted widespread support. Hayes called for a separate organisation within the Unitarian General Assembly, for special meetings within the Annual Meetings of the movement, and for Unitarian chapels to change their name to the Church of the Great Companions. 'Unitarians of the United World must make their presence felt in our community', he argued (Hayes, 1938a: 6). Such an approach was not in keeping with the Liberal Christian majority view of the day, and he would not have endeared himself to denominational leaders.

Secondly, Hayes produced a lot of work on the teachings and philosophies of other religions, but they tended not to be critical and analytical, even though his books claimed to be studies in Comparative Religion. Some of his statements and assumptions are naïve, especially his belief that all the religions could be synthesised into agreed basic tenets. 'It is possible to see all the religions as a whole...as sects of some greater religion of humanity' (Hayes, 1938a: 21). He was able to synthesise the religions because he assessed them according to his own criteria for religion. He presented their beliefs according to the categories of *God, scripture, life after death,* and *salvation.* Within all the major religions he found a doctrine to satisfy each of these categories, with no acknowledgement that what a Western Christian may find significant may not be the case for others. For example, the 'Changeless Essence of Change' in Buddhism was equated with the Christian 'God' and the Islamic 'Allah' (Hayes, 1938a: 23).

Thirdly, much of his research was flawed. He had little contact with living representatives of other religions and tended to misrepresent them. He quite freely used Christian words and ideas and transplanted them to other religions. Thus, Krishna was 'the Christ of India' (Hayes, 1931a: 36), the Indian sacred texts were 'Bibles' (p. 9) and the Buddha was a 'saint' and 'Saviour' (Hayes, 1931b: 23). Furthermore, Hayes relied on a great deal of secondary sources. *Sweet Calumus,* for example, a book of only 44 pages, uses no fewer than 25 secondary sources (Hayes, 1931c). This is not to say that Hayes did not take a scholarly approach, but that his findings were heavily dependent on the interpretation of ancient documents by other scholars.

In later chapters I will comment on Hayes' contribution to the adoption of ideas and beliefs from other religions into Unitarianism. Despite what I have said about his work on Comparative Religion, however, there is no doubt that he made a tremendous contribution. He produced more than thirty publications, most of them collections of stories from different traditions or comparisons of symbols and parables, such as *Leaves from the Larger Bible* (1929). He wrote services of worship containing material drawn from all traditions (1954) and he edited sacred poems and meditations written by others, such as the translations of the Tamil poet, Thayumanavar (1932).

Hayes' contribution to Comparative Religion in British Unitarianism should be acknowledged for several reasons. Firstly, he was effective in making the beliefs of other religions accessible to British Unitarians. Whereas before a great effort had been required to secure appropriate material on which to reflect, Hayes now provided suitable material in easily readable small units. For ministers wishing to use such material in worship, Hayes' work was ideal, in that modern translations were used, and material was categorised according to themes that were common in Unitarian worship of the day, such as 'True Religion' (Hayes, 1954: 59), 'At-One-Ment or Atonement' (Hayes, 1929: 43), and 'The Friendship of All Creatures' (Hayes, 1938b: 21). His works were easy to read, with many complex doctrines being presented in slim booklets, their ideas carefully explained and often illustrated by diagrams, charts, and pictures (Hayes, 1938a, 1938b).

Secondly, Hayes was genuinely innovative in arguing for an appreciation of the feminine in religion. In examining the religious traditions of other countries, he came to the conclusion that most religions acknowledged a divine feminine principle, referred to in his work as 'the Great Mother' (Hayes, undated: 3). As various religions worshipped the feminine in the form of Isis, Ishtar, Prithivi, and Kwan Yin, Hayes argued that the feminine aspect of God had broken through into Christianity, the Virgin Mary taking that role (Hayes, undated: 4). As the older religions witnessed to the feminine aspect of God in so many ways, Hayes argued that the religion of tomorrow had equally to adopt a feminine form of the Godhead.

We must bring the conception of the Motherhood of God back into man's thought...so that men and women will know each other aright...without striving to crush, to subdue, to usurp, to separate. (Hayes, undated: 10)

Thirdly, a contribution that will be explored in a later chapter, is Hayes' distinctive use of the findings of Comparative Religion. The discoveries in other religions were to have a practical effect. The absorption of knowledge about the other religions of the world was intended to broaden the sphere of pastoral activity, not only as far as the ministry was concerned, but for the Unitarian movement as a whole. Following the death of Carpenter there was no other British Unitarian who made such a contribution to Comparative Religion.

Other British Unitarian contributions

The contributions of several other British Unitarians should not be overlooked.

Travers Herford was a student of ancient Hebrew religion, held in high esteem by Jewish scholars for producing the first unbiased study of Judaism of two thousand years ago (Goring and Goring, 1984: 55). His writings are said to have influenced modern liberal Jewish scholarship (Chryssides, 1998: 77).

Herbert Crabtree (1889–1982), a minister, was probably the first Unitarian to write critically on the new religions. Dealing with Christian Science, Theosophy, and Spiritualism, he did not so much compare the teachings of those religions with Unitarianism as point out those areas where Unitarians would have some sympathy, such as a concern for religious discipline and interest in evidence for life after death (Crabtree, 1932: 30). His treatment of Theosophy was not very sympathetic, but he did raise awareness of the movement among Unitarians, and in later years there have been Unitarian ministers, and probably a number of laypeople too, who have combined membership of the Theosophical Society with their Unitarianism. George W. Parkinson (1906–1983) was for many years a leading member of a Theosophical lodge in Scarborough during his ministry there. Eric Breeze, currently ministering to the Hyde Chapel and Flowery Field Church, also in Hyde, is a long-standing Theosophist.

It was a British Unitarian who pioneered the teaching of Comparative Religion in Indian schools. **Margaret Barr** (1897–1973) spent years working among the Assamese people on several enterprises. As an experiment in a Calcutta girls' school from 1933 to 1936, she created her own course of studies, objectively considering the different religious traditions of India and comparing them with Christianity. The course was later produced as a textbook and is a model of objectivity (Barr, 1937).

Although it was now considered essential for British Unitarians to engage with ideas, beliefs, and philosophies of other religions, it is surprising that their own contributions in later years should be so sparse. Apart from a few minor articles in various journals, nothing of any substance was produced until 1990, when **David Doel** published his *The Perennial Psychology* (Doel, 1990). This was not intended as a study in Comparative Religion as such, but as the presentation of the psychology complementing the 'Perennial Philosophy' that Aldous Huxley (1894–1963) had derived from the ideas of Leibnitz and which he discovered within the mystical or contemplative traditions in the great religions of the world. Doel's book contained, nevertheless, many comparisons of theories and techniques of modern depth psychology with the great contemplative traditions of the different world religions. Whole chapters, along with useful charts, dealt with the similarities between the traditions on, for example, concepts of death, despair, and rebirth.

Dr Doel followed up this book with *Out of Clouds and Darkness* (1992), a work that explored the relationships between religious and psychotherapeutic teachings with reference to several of life's crises, using, once again, material culled from the world's great religions. *The Lost Child and the Christ Child* (1997) similarly used such material to elaborate the great themes of contemplative theology and modern depth psychology within the simple model of the Lost Child and the Christ Child, derived from the myth of St Christopher.

Doel's comparative studies were not directly related to Unitarianism. This was not the case, however, with the work of a Unitarian lay academic, **George Chryssides**. Currently a Senior Lecturer in Religious Studies at the University of Wolverhampton, Dr Chryssides has produced work on specific world religions, such as his book on Buddhism (1988). He has taken a special interest, however, in 'New Religious Movements'. Furthermore, he has considered the impact of the ideas of such movements on British Unitarianism. In one of his works, for example, he listed the various features of new religious movements that are unappealing to Unitarians, including fanaticism, unreason, authority, Biblicism, traditional forms of atonement, and alienation from the world (Chryssides, 1999: 96-8). He then demonstrated how Unitarians could be attracted to so-called 'New Age' movements by their rejection of institutional religion, their lack of any agreed creed, and the absence of any authoritative hierarchy (p. 100). In a later article, Chryssides considered whether Unitarianism was 'restorative', seeking to recover a supposed lost past as the Jehovah's Witnesses do in their claim to be reconstructing primordial Christianity, or whether it was 'innovative', as is the Unification Church with its belief that past prophets received only partial revelations (Chryssides, 2002: 32-3). The significance of Chryssides' work is that it recognised the new readiness of some Unitarians to absorb some of the values, beliefs, and principles of modern religious movements that have emerged from totally contrasting traditions, as will be explored in a later chapter.

The current position

The importance of the study of world religions for British Unitarianism is demonstrated by its status as an essential component of the various education and training programmes of the movement. The training programme for lay people, for those seeking accreditation as lay preachers, and those who choose a more academic course, includes a module on the Study of World Religions (Marshall, 2003) of a length and depth equal to those on Biblical Studies, Unitarian Thought, and Unitarian History. The course is partly comparative, in that it seeks to approach the different religions by reflecting on their sacred texts, prominent figures, and festivals, and by comparing them with Unitarian ideas (Marshall, 2003: 5-6).

The two English colleges responsible for the training of Unitarian ministers also give instruction on some aspect of the study of World Religions in their curricula. This is at least partly due to the requirements of the denomination, as World Religions is one of the six academic disciplines considered essential for training for the ministry (General Assembly, 1995:7). Harris Manchester College usually expects its students to pursue a degree course provided by the University of Oxford, as the college is now a full member of that University. For most students this means studying for a Bachelor of Theology degree that has a World Religions element in it. For those who pursue other options, World Religions is taught as part of the pastoral training, when up to eight different world religions are studied. Notably the Harris Manchester course still retains a comparative study. It seeks to analyse other religions in accordance with what is of significance to a Western believer from a Christian tradition. Thus, emphasis is laid on the founders, sacred texts, and doctrines about God, immortality, and the source of evil (Harris Manchester College, 1995: 10). The assumption, firstly, is that there are identifiable founders. In some cases, such as Hinduism, this would be difficult to ascertain. The second assumption is that other religions have a notion of God. Whether Taoism, Confucianism, or Buddhism, all featured on Harris Manchester's list, can be thought of as being theistic is a matter of great debate. The same objection can be raised about immortality. The main difficulty with Harris Manchester's approach is that it views other religions through the eyes of a Western Christian believer. What is considered important and central to the followers of those religions is not what is studied primarily. Instead, the approach asks what is important to the student, and how someone from a Christian perspective can find parallels in those religions being studied.

The Unitarian College is in a similar position regarding its relationship with the neighbouring University of Manchester. For students who undertake a degree course under the aegis of the Partnership for Theological Education, formerly the Northern Federation for Training in Ministry, a course in World Religions is available, although it makes up less than ten per cent of the entire degree content. Its focus is principally on dialogue and on issues connected with pastoral concerns. There is an academic study of another religion, although it approaches the subject through issues significant to Christianity rather than encountering the religion on its own terms (Northern Federation, 1997: 55).

My survey conducted among British Unitarian ministers and lay leaders demonstrated that there are very few who have not studied World Religions. Of the 80 who returned their questionnaires, 25 had studied the subject at degree level and 18 at postgraduate level. The most astonishing figure is the 51 respondents who declared that they had studied some aspect of World Religions as a private study. No fewer than 69 of the respondents affirmed that they brought the teachings of other religions into their preaching, and that they used their sacred texts and works of other religious leaders.

Conclusion

As can be seen in this chapter, British Unitarianism has considered that the study of the world's religions is of great importance, and this importance has grown in the twentieth century and into the new millennium. It is helpful at this stage to consider why such a study has been considered vital to British Unitarians.

Firstly, there is a proven need within the movement to use the resources of world religions in order to find a new theology or a basic principle. In terms of religious belief, British Unitarianism contains very little that all its devotees can share. The General Assembly, in its newly adopted Object, promotes 'a free and inquiring religion through the worship of God and the celebration of life…and the upholding of the liberal Christian tradition' (Gilley, 2002: 4). Exactly what those words mean, however, is for the interpretation of the individual, as they have become historical language symbols rather than points of belief. A revised edition of *Beliefs of a Unitarian*, published in 1962, stated that 'Unitarians believe first of all and most profoundly in God' (Hall, 1962: 21). Attached to this statement, however, was a footnote by one of the editors, pointing out that there are Unitarians in Britain who would strongly dissent from that view, describing themselves as humanists who do not feel that the object of their worship is personal. The reference in the Object to the upholding of the liberal Christian tradition suggests a respect for the past, rather than a reflection of the current position. Only 25 out of the 80 responses received from those ministers and lay leaders who returned their questionnaires considered themselves Liberal Christians. According to a survey of more than a thousand Unitarian women, conducted in 2001, just over 40 per cent considered themselves 'Christian-based' (Gilley, 2002: 15). That leaves almost 60 per cent who are not. For that larger section of the movement, there is no coherent tenet to hold them together.

For those Unitarians who do not describe themselves as Christians, a greater interest in the world's religions is apparent. This is evidenced by those ministers and lay leaders who participated in the survey. Dr Richard Boeke, for example, currently Secretary of the World Congress of Faiths, is a frequent attender at conferences of the International Association for Religious Freedom, and studied World Religions to postgraduate level. To him, no religion can be superior to any other, as they are all different responses to the same spiritual reality (Boeke, 1996: 4). For such an individual, Unitarianism has become a post-Christian movement and needs the resources of other religions to help individual Unitarians to recognise the reality of the oneness of religion (Boeke, 2003: 3). For Unitarians, the study of other religions is important in order that the movement can act as a bridge, 'linking religions and even atheists in the common quest for a future worth living' (Boeke, 2002: 25).

The second reason why some Unitarians find the study of World Religions valuable is because it reaffirms them in their Christian faith (Midgley, 1975: 107). It entails a process by which the individual, when confronted with valid insights from other traditions, is able to rediscover what is important in his or her own faith. This process, what William

Hocking (1873–1966) called 'reconception', does not mean abandoning one's own faith but pushes one to examine one's own more deeply and search beyond the peripheral to what is more fundamental (Hocking, 1940: 192). Rev. Arthur Long was for 14 years the Principal of the Unitarian College, Manchester. In that time he made certain that Comparative Religion, as it was then known, was an integral part of the College curriculum, long before any instruction from the General Assembly. Arthur Long, however, was a keen Unitarian Christian, a long-time officer of the Unitarian Christian Association and former editor of its Journal. For him, the study of other religions, and the consequent theological diversity within Unitarianism, was an opportunity to test one's own Christian commitment. 'I devoutly hope that I shall always be ready to listen gladly to the arguments of those who challenge my own assumptions' (Long, 1982: 12).

The third reason for the importance accorded to the study of World Religions by British Unitarians is that many ministers see themselves as 'Inter-Faith' ministers. This idea was promoted by a minister living in a multi-ethnic and multi-religious community who considered his ministry as being of service to all those in the vicinity, regardless of their religious background (Benton, 1978). Many inter-faith weddings have been celebrated in Unitarian chapels (Simons, 1985: 28); in service books such as *Celebrating Life* (Hill, 1993), texts for weddings have been provided from other religious sources, not only for Unitarians interested in using non-Christian material, but also for use by couples from different religious backgrounds. *Celebrating Life* was a great contrast to the older *Book of Occasional Services* (General Assembly, 1932b), which used no material from other religions but presented a liberal Christian format with occasional use of poetry or secular readings. In order to provide such a service, there is a need to understand something of the doctrines and traditions of the religion in question.

Comparative Religion (or, more correctly, the Study of World Religions) has long been of great importance to British Unitarianism – and not as a mere academic exercise. For more than a hundred years, British Unitarians have sought to give a practical edge to their interest in other religions. Thus, in the next chapter, consideration will be given to the contribution made by British Unitarians to inter-religious dialogue. Once again, the efforts of such work will be evaluated in the consequential theological and pastoral changes experienced by contemporary British Unitarians.

3 Inter-religious dialogue

Introduction

The first chapter set the scene for the study as a whole. The second chapter considered the contribution of British Unitarians to the academic study of world religions. This chapter now examines the contribution of British Unitarians to inter-religious dialogue. It considers the three radically different attempts of British Unitarians to create a meaningful way of securing working relations with other religions. First, it presents the Informal Approach, whereby links with other religions were established on a personal or *ad hoc* basis. The Institutional Approach is then examined, assessing the contribution of British Unitarians to the work of the inter-religious bodies that were formed following the 1893 Parliament of the World's Religions. The chapter then considers the phenomenon of the Dual-Adherence Approach, whereby British Unitarians who, having found value in another religious movement, then become more closely attached to it, alongside their continuing Unitarian connections.

The Informal Approach

The letter to the Moroccan Ambassador

The first apparent attempt by British Unitarians to establish links with other religions was a letter written to the Moroccan Ambassador to London in 1682 (Primary Document, 1892: 523). The two writers of the letter claimed to represent the Unitarian denomination and pointed out that the Unitarian belief in the unity of the Godhead and rejection of Trinitarianism were akin to the Islamic view of an undivided God. The ambassador, Ahmet ben Abdullah, being a state official of his country, and aware of the religious nature of the letter, refused to accept it – and thus the project failed to get under way (Chryssides, 1998: 68).

The significance of the letter, however, needs to be examined for the following reasons. Firstly, the writers were anonymous, and no attempt to identify them has ever been successful. Whoever they were, they were acting on their own initiative and not officially representing any movement of people called Unitarians. Secondly, there was no religious movement in Britain at that time called 'Unitarian'. There were individual congregations that could be considered, retrospectively, as holding to a Unitarian theological position, but there was no congregation bearing the name of Unitarian until 1774, when Theophilus Lindsey founded the Essex Chapel in London (Gow, 1928: 90-92). A structured denomination bearing the name Unitarian was not created until 1825, when the British and Foreign Unitarian Association came into existence.

The significance of the letter lies in the fact that it does appear to represent the will of Unitarians through the ages to establish inter-religious links. Without greater clarity about its origins and status, however, it is debateable how far it can be recognised as a genuine early attempt at establishing links between Unitarianism and another world religion.

Lant Carpenter (1780–1840) and Mary Carpenter (1807–1877)

One of the most celebrated British Unitarians in his day, Lant Carpenter, mentioned already in the previous chapter, was a minister who combined his pastoral work with careers as an educationalist and social reformer. His links with Indian religion derived from his contacts with Rammohun Roy, founder of the Brahmo Samaj. Before visiting Britain in 1833, Roy contacted Carpenter, considering him to be one of the leading Unitarians of his time. Carpenter believed Roy's search for a pure monotheism within the ancient scriptures of India was admirable, and that it could lead to the establishment of Unitarian Christianity in that country.

Although Roy died soon after arriving in Britain, Lant Carpenter kept up his links with India, as recorded in a book written by his son (R. L. Carpenter, 1848). One of the consequences of the relationship was the enthusiasm for all things Indian demonstrated by Lant's daughter, Mary Carpenter, who was inspired to visit India four times. She went principally to examine the country's social institutions, but while there she developed relationships with mainstream Hindus who befriended her in order to develop philanthropic institutions (W. B. Carpenter, 1877: 17). She examined the links between the teachings of Hinduism and its social expression and sought to make Hindus adopt a practical approach to their religion. Her book about Roy demonstrated her belief that links between Britain and India could bring out the importance of the social and ethical dimension of religious practice (M. Carpenter, 1875). This led her to establish a relationship with Keshab Chandra Sen (1838–1884), the leader of the Brahmo Samaj, many years after Roy's death. Sen is cited as being the inspiration behind Mary Carpenter's founding of the National Indian Association (Sargant, 1987).

The contributions of Lant and Mary Carpenter are important in two respects. Firstly, there was an early development towards promotion of a universalist view of religion. Lant Carpenter identified with Roy's universalist convictions: they both believed that all religions stemmed from a common monotheistic root. Lant Carpenter's book, *On Rajah Rammohun Roy* (1833), detailed his many links with the Brahmo Samaj and heralded Roy as a possible creator of inter-religious initiatives in India. Mary Carpenter's relationship with Sen is important in that he too had a universalist view, seeking a merger of some Indian ideas with Christian teaching, a practice that some later Unitarians would emulate.

Secondly, Unitarians were gradually moving towards a definition of religion in ethical terms. Their later co-operation with the International Association for Religious Freedom (IARF) was concerned less with doctrinal and theological issues than with issues of social and national ethics (Traer, 2000: 4). As will be considered later in this chapter, the apparent focus of the IARF on liberal Christian theological issues is what inspired some British Unitarians to seek involvement in inter-religious dialogue elsewhere. The British and Foreign Unitarian Association in its early years also promoted the idea of 'Domestic Missions' to ease social misery and to seek social justice (Mellone, 1925: 108). The example of the Carpenters demonstrates the positive consequences of early informal inter-religious relations.

Robert Spears (1825–1899)

In many ways Spears' career was a contrast to the Carpenters' initiatives. He had no wish to merge Hindu and Christian ideas. He did, however, believe firmly that, by establishing links with other believers, individuals could clarify their own faith, and to this end he did make contact with liberal Hindus (Carter, 1902: 114). Formerly a lay New Connexion

Methodist, Spears became a well-respected Unitarian minister and rose to become, for nine years, Co-Secretary of the British and Foreign Unitarian Association and editor of several denominational journals (Ruston, 1999: 54-9). Spears held to traditional Unitarian theology based on the centrality of the Bible. In fact, he believed the Bible to be thoroughly Unitarian in all its teachings from beginning to end. For the New Testament in particular he had a great passion (Ruston, 2003: 1).

For Spears, Unitarianism would always be a Bible-based liberal Christian denomination. In fact, he resigned his position as Co-Secretary of the British and Foreign Unitarian Association when it agreed to republish a book by Theodore Parker (1810–1860), *A Discourse of Matters Pertaining to Religion* (1876), which was considered an attack on Biblical Unitarianism. The event was a major turning point in British Unitarian history, marking the fact that a broader type of Unitarianism was now the orthodoxy. 'The pure doctrine of Biblical Unitarianism was dead' (Thomas, 1969: 113).

It must be asked at this point why Spears was an instigator of inter-religious dialogue when, unlike many of his Unitarian colleagues, he saw his role as being to propagate Unitarian Christianity rather than seek a theological compromise. The answer lies in his distinctive approach to Christianity. Spears believed that Christianity was neither a culture-bound nor complex religion. The teachings of Jesus, he believed, were simple and practical. He sought to establish inter-religious dialogue for several reasons. Firstly, by discovering the ethical basis of one's faith one could recognise in Christianity something with a universal appeal. He thus established close contact with the Brahmo Samaj and contributed to the success of Keshab Chandra Sen's visit to Britain (Charlesworth, 1903: 13-14). Spears thereby sought to give a more attractive face to the Christianity that he espoused.

Secondly, Spears quite shamelessly established links with other believers in order to spread his own Unitarian view of Jesus. He was so confident of his position that he had no doubts that his form of Unitarian Christianity would eventually be triumphant. He believed that liberal Hindus were so knowledgeable about the teachings of Jesus that it would take little persuasion to encourage them to accept the Christian tradition as the true path. Thirdly, he was genuinely interested in the diversity of religious expression. He was not prone to minimise the differences between the religions, but was interested in what could be learned from them. 'It is not our differences which separate us in life, so much as the way we handle them', he wrote (1899: 135-6).

Joseph Estlin Carpenter (1844–1927)

Carpenter has already been mentioned in the previous chapter. At this juncture, however, it is important to mention that he did seek to understand other religions through personal contacts. Carpenter was grandson of the aforementioned Lant Carpenter and nephew of Mary Carpenter. His father, William Benjamin Carpenter (1812–1885), was a distinguished biologist and academic at the University of London. Estlin Carpenter studied for the pastoral ministry and then took up ministerial duties at the Oakfield Road Church in Bristol from 1866 to 1869, before moving to Mill Hill Chapel, Leeds. In 1876 he joined the staff of Manchester New College, eventually becoming its Principal. It was while he was there that he undertook most of his studies in Biblical scholarship and Comparative Religion. He was recognised in his age as one of the major figures in British Unitarianism (Holt, 1938: 338). He became a Pali scholar and a commentator on the sacred texts of most of the great religions, but particularly those of Buddhism and Hinduism.

What was important for this discussion was his determination to develop and maintain links with active adherents of other religions. In 1910 he attended the International Congress for Free Christianity and Religious Progress, attended, for the first time, by substantial numbers of adherents of other world religions. Carpenter's association with them made him aware of their mutual concern for the social order and the foundations of morality. He believed that they could have a major influence upon the powers that shaped civilisation (1910: 4).

Carpenter had no contacts at this time with traditional Hindu believers. He was in touch, however, with members of the Brahmo Samaj, which he considered to be an authentic expression of Hinduism. This was because it linked modern Indians with the dawn of history, even though it sought to harmonise Indian and Western ideals. He was closely enough identified with them to be asked to address the movement on its eighty-second anniversary (1912). What attracted him to the Brahmo Samaj was its repudiation of images and of the doctrine of *karma*, and its adherence to an ethical position more in keeping with Christian moral values (1912: 7).

Carpenter also had links with other Indian teachers whose radicalism led them out of traditional Hinduism. He was in regular correspondence, for example, with the social reformer, Sasipada Banerjee (1842–1925), the founder of the Devalaya Church Institute, a freethinking and non-dogmatic organisation with Hindu origins (Farnell, 1929: 178). Carpenter became a regular contributor to its *Quarterly Journal,* a periodical that was first published in 1918. Carpenter was also in touch with, and vigorously debated with, a figure called Alokananda Mahabharati of Behar. Mahabharati was a follower of a religious leader known as Thakur Dayananda Deb, who believed that the day was close at hand when the people of the world could be united into a formal union. Carpenter scorned such a belief by asserting that the time was far from ripe for such a development (Herford, 1929: 83). With another freethinking Hindu called Togendra Ghose of Calcutta, Carpenter shared his views on the need to create a network of friends who 'shunned superstitions'. They would also seek the creation of a religious system based on simple theistic principles and devoid of what they deemed unnecessary doctrines such as that of the Trinity (*ibid.*: 29). As can be seen, Carpenter had a number of significant contacts with Indian thinkers, although it is clear that he tended to seek out those whose religious position was congenial to Unitarians.

Carpenter had further contacts with Indian believers by means of his support for the new Indian Unitarian movement, founded in North East India in 1887 (Sparham, 1946: 6). Although founded by a convert from Calvinism, the movement was active within tribal animistic communities and thus had more in common with indigenous traditions and with Indian monotheism than with Christianity (Lyngdoh, 1987: 9).

Carpenter also visited Palestine, and his letters from there indicated that he had made contacts and from them had developed an appreciation of the Islamic religion (1873). Furthermore, Carpenter's biographer suggested that Japanese scholars highly esteemed his work, and that he maintained friendly relations with a number of oriental teachers (Farnell, 1929: 178).

The modern era

British Unitarianism in the modern era has continued to further informal links with adherents of the world's religions, although some of those links have developed into a structured form. In the survey connected with this research, 45 of the 80 ministers and lay leaders who returned their questionnaires claimed attendance at the places of worship of other religions, with 26 claiming to work on joint campaigns on social and political issues (see Appendix 1). Some Unitarians have made it their particular role to further relationships with other religions. The late Alfred Benton (1906–2000), for example, served a Unitarian congregation in the heart of the predominantly Asian community of Small Heath in Birmingham. During his ministry he promoted strong relations with the Sikh community, who used the church hall for large religious gatherings. Particularly distinctive in Benton's approach was his engagement with individual Sikhs on a non-doctrinal level. There were no formal discussions of religious differences and similarities. Instead, the facilities of the congregation were offered as an act of friendship, with the hope that mutual understanding would come from regular fellowship.

> *There are great opportunities for valuable work in these areas, especially when personal relationships have been developed between individuals, where labels have been relegated to the background, where people are just people.*
> (Benton, 1978:10)

Unitarians have consistently sought to establish closer but informal links with other believers. In the 1970s and 1980s the late Rev. John Robbins (1915–1987), minister for some years to London's Newington Green and Islington congregations, was noted for his liberal Jewish connections, while Rev. Kenneth Ridgway, now retired and living in Leeds, even spent two years studying at the Leo Baeck Seminary, the liberal Jewish rabbinical college (General Assembly, 2003: 72). In the 1990s, meetings took place at a national level between Unitarians and Muslims and between Unitarians and Sufis, in order to deepen mutual understanding and to find common ground (Marshall, 1999: 54). During that same period a number of congregations invited believers of other religions to visit their churches to talk about their beliefs and practices (*ibid.*). The consequence of such close links has meant, in some cases, a departure from the Unitarian movement in order to join another religion (Dickinson, 1984: 6-8). In fact, the Bahá'í faith has actually sought out new converts directly by appealing in Unitarian publications to the similarities between it and Unitarianism (Firoozmand, 1984: 9-10).

As can be seen, the informal relationships between Unitarians and followers of other religions have had an impact that has influenced the way in which Unitarianism has developed and how it continues to conduct itself. A strengthening of the trend towards a more integrationist form of Unitarianism was to come about, however, following the greater involvement of Unitarians in formal inter-religious institutions.

The Institutional Approach

The Informal Approach to inter-religious dialogue has not always proved to be sufficient for British Unitarians. For more than one hundred years, Unitarians in Britain have taken an active role in the development of, and participation in, formal inter-religious bodies. It was a Unitarian minister originally from Wales, though at the time working in the USA, Jenkin Lloyd Jones (1843–1918), who was one of the three co-organisers of the 1893 World's Parliament of Religions. Estlin Carpenter, a major supporter of the notion of inter-religious dialogue, wrote a paper to be delivered to the Parliament (1893), although he was unable to attend and had his paper read on his behalf (Braybrooke, 1992: 34). Inspired by the work of the Parliament, the world's first international inter-religious organisation was founded in 1900. Now known as the International Association for Religious Freedom, it was then known as the International Council of Unitarian and Other Liberal Religious Thinkers and Workers. The major reason for its existence was quite specific.

> *The object of this council is to open communication with those in all lands who are striving to unite Pure Religion and Perfect Liberty, and to increase fellowship and cooperation among them.* (Wendte, 1907: 1)

Estlin Carpenter was its first President, and a major contributor to its regular international congresses. The second Secretary was Rev. Dr. William Hamilton Drummond (1863–1945), another leading British Unitarian (Godfrey, 1999: 7). Since then, British Unitarians have continued to hold office in the organisation, have contributed to its meetings, and have dominated the membership of what is now known as the British Chapter of the organisation, a part of the IARF structure that was formed in 1962 (*ibid.*: 12).

Hope for a convergence of religions

As Unitarians were very much involved in the IARF, one must wonder why it was then felt necessary by British Unitarians to be involved with other, apparently competing, organisations that sought inter-religious dialogue. For example, a short-lived Fellowship of Faiths was created in the 1920s, partly run by Will Hayes (Hayes, 1954: 8). Also, an Inter-Religious Fellowship was organised in 1930 by Leslie Belton (1897–1949) (Peacock, 1956: 11), a Unitarian minister and editor of the Unitarian newspaper, *The Inquirer*. A number of Unitarians were involved either in setting up, or helping to run, the World Congress of Faiths (WCF), the inter-religious organisation founded in 1936. These included, as well as Hayes (Hayes, 1954: 8), Arthur Peacock (1905–1968), a former Universalist minister, who joined the Unitarian movement following the demise of the Universalist Church (Braybrooke, 1992: 72). Peacock was to serve as the Secretary of the WCF for a number of years. Other leaders of the WCF included very prominent Unitarians, such as the two politicians, Reginald Sorensen (1891–1971) and James Chuter Ede (1881–1965). Today another Unitarian, Rev. Dr. Richard Boeke, is its Secretary. It must be asked whether there was thus something about the IARF that encouraged British Unitarians to seek involvement in other organisations promoting inter-religious dialogue.

What is noticeable about the position of these British Unitarians is that they looked to a convergence of the religions into one all-embracing faith. This had been the vision of Jenkin Lloyd Jones: 'Let us build a temple of universal religion dedicated to the inquiring spirit of progress, to the helpful service of love' (Seager, 1986: 205-6). Estlin Carpenter, an evolutionist, believed that each religion represented a different stage of evolutionary progress, and that Unitarianism was the most advanced in the present age. Ultimately, however, a new religion would emerge to unite all the religions of the world, at a time that he referred to as 'the day of mutual understanding' (1893: 849).

That this approach had some kind of credibility is attested by the many speeches suggesting something similar at the 1893 Parliament of the World's Religions. One example is the paper delivered by a prominent Jewish rabbi and scholar who, while scorning universalistic claims of religions such as Buddhism, Islam, and Christianity, argued that the universal religion was still to come and was humankind's destiny.

*Race and nationality cannot circumscribe the fellowship of the larger
communion of the faithful, a communion destined to embrace in one
covenant all the children of man.* (Hirsch, 1893:1304)

Within British Unitarianism several prominent ministers had perpetuated
this approach. Hayes had made this quite clear with his Order of the Great
Companions: 'The line of evolution in our faith is towards World Religion'
(1938a: 5). Peacock's motto was a verse from the work of Elizabeth Barrett
Browning: 'Universalism – universe religion – the unity of all things, why
it's the greatest word in our language' (Braybrooke, 1992:72). Sorensen
sought a new religion, a 'modern faith' that would take in the best of all
elements to be found within the world's religions and would embrace
science and social progress – a concept pursued in his book, *I Believe in
Man* (1970). It had seemed that the IARF would not be the vehicle for the
realisation of this hope. Although the organisation included participants
from Jewish, Muslim, Hindu, and Roman Catholic communities, it was
Protestant communities and Unitarian Christians that dominated it. Its
1910 Congress heard celebrated theologians who were almost exclusively
Christian, and in 1936 its then Dutch leader, seeing religious development
in evolutionary terms with Christianity at its apex, made clear that one of
the major aims of the organisation was to promulgate 'Free Christianity'.

*We realise that it has to fulfil a real task in the present world situation. This
task is not only to unite the liberal Christians and other religious Liberals the
world over, but to give testimony of what Free Christianity is and strives
after.* (Faber, 1936: 3)

It was not until 1949 that the IARF addressed issues that did not include
specific references to Christianity and sought to be wholly inclusive (Traer,
2000: 4). It was as late as 1969, at its Boston Congress, that the final
change was made to its current name, a name that omits specific reference to Christianity and offers 'no suggestion of specialisation' (Bell,
1970: 29). Many more non-Christian bodies have since joined, although
they tend to be from the liberal end of the religious spectrum within their
own traditions (Braybrooke, 1992: 61).

For some British Unitarians, the emphasis on Liberal Christianity in the
IARF hindered them from seeking, within inter-religious dialogue, the
vision of a convergence of the religions into one all-embracing religion,

and they sought to achieve their hopes through membership of other bodies. There are reasons, however, why the IARF could not have survived if it had sought the convergence of religions as its guiding principle. Firstly, there is the inference that reason could overcome the differences between the religions. This suggests that convergence would come about after an agreement on *ideas*. The rich and diverse practices of the communities that have given shape to religious traditions would then appear to be superfluous. It is difficult to think of the different religions as being bound up with sets of ideas. Such an approach assumes that each world religion is a carefully packaged unit, with a coherent and identifiable set of teachings. It dismisses the reality of the personal faith experiences of its adherents. Wilfred Cantwell Smith (1916–2000) dealt with this issue in *The Meaning and End of Religion* (1978), where he spoke of 'personal faith' and 'cumulative tradition' in preference to 'religion'.

A second difficulty with the idea of convergence is that what some religions consider as fundamental is treated by others as of marginal concern. The recognition of a universal religious consciousness, the faculty that would be tapped in order to create a future universal religion, could be acknowledged as little more than an absolutising of one's own beliefs. It could mean that the adherents of one religion will equate their vision of the truth with *the* truth – leaving themselves open to the charge of inadvertent dogmatism.

The vision of a convergence of the religions having been rejected, the IARF needed a new basis on which to carry out its work. The organisation had always placed social and ethical concerns at the centre of its activities. The 1907 Congress, addressed by Julia Ward Howe (1819–1910), considered how the social values now being adopted by the inter-faith movement had played its part in the abolition of slavery. The Congress then committed itself to the pursuit of social righteousness and 'perfect liberty' (Eliot, 1907: 48). The organisation has continued since then to give social and ethical values a high priority. This is not to say that the other inter-religious organisations have ignored social concerns. On the contrary, many of them have collaborated to promote shared aims. An example of this was the declaration of 1993 as the Year of Inter-Religious Understanding and Co-operation.

The issues of ethical and social justice have now become paramount as aims of the IARF, since the vision of convergence has faded. There are certainly no signs of a growing organic merger of the religions. In fact, there are developments that could be interpreted as contradictory signs. There is a growing exclusivism in branches of the major religions, manifested in some cases in extreme violent behaviour. Nonetheless, the religions are encountering one another to a degree that was not possible a hundred years ago. There are no signs of doctrinal unity, no eschewing of those elements of religion believed necessary in order to bring closer the ideal religion of the future. Much inter-religious work in the modern era has been directed, not towards a rejection of the uniqueness of one's tradition, but towards a greater appreciation of it.

> *If we engage in the hermeneutics of inter-faith dialogue, we may find a more meaningful and creative understanding of our own tradition. That is to say, through inter-religious dialogue we Buddhists are on the way to being better Buddhists in the same way that Christians are on the way to being better Christians.* (Nemoto, 1999: 11)

A new understanding of revelation

For British Unitarians inspired by Carpenter, the inter-religious movement was where a new revelation could be discovered, clarified by an avoidance of concentration on the particularities of individual religious traditions. Carpenter believed that the religions could come together to discover jointly a revelation of the divine within their individual teachings on ethics, inspiration, and incarnation (1893). Such a universal acknowledgement within the world's different religious traditions would, he felt, bring about recognition that the heritage of the world's religions was the heritage of all. Hayes also spoke of a 'cosmic consciousness' that transcended religious particularities, which could be discovered when there was an acknowledgement of the value of the resources and traditions of all religions (1938a: 64). Thus, inter-religious dialogue was about searching for, and being open to, that universal revelatory communication that could speak anew to all peoples.

The difficulty with such an approach is that revelation is so often restricted to something discovered within the sacred writings of the religions. Several problems then arise. Firstly, there is the insurmountable problem of detaching a doctrine from its religious and cultural packaging. Revelation for some traditions is inextricably connected with a concept that is alien to others. It is difficult to isolate something that may be accepted by all from a philosophical tool that to all but the adherents of that religion is a conundrum. The Hindu concept of the *trimurti*, its association with other gods, and their identification as the hidden self or *atman*, as detailed in the Maitri Upanishad (5, 1-2), is a form of revelatory teaching that would appal those, especially mainstream Christians, who envisage a clear separation between God and humanity. The Buddhist teaching on the achievement of *nirvana*, the loss of identification with the self, a state beyond existence and non-existence, is a vital element of that religion. This was something that happened to the Buddha himself, the *parinirvana*, as indicated in the Majjhima Nikaya (245-6). Again, such vital revelatory teaching is unacceptable to some traditions, Christianity included, which believes that revelation has confirmed the reality of the continuation of the individual self, although there are adherents of a 'negative theology' expressed by such writers as Meister Eckhart (1260–1327) and John of the Cross (1542–1591) (Bowden, 1990: 42, 67).

Secondly, if revelation is to be a notion shared by the world's religions, then the question arises: which scriptures are to be acknowledged as authoritative? The question of divine inspiration, and to what extent it can be considered as infallible, has divided the Christian community for a very long time. Other traditions, such as Islam, have yet to face this issue for themselves before the world community can begin to accept a common approach to written revelation.

It is difficult to understand why the notion of revelation should be restricted to the written word. Carpenter himself admitted the significance of direct revelation in his own life, when he enjoyed a mystical experience while walking in the Welsh mountains. 'The sense of a direct relation to God then generated in my soul has become a part of my habitual thought and feeling' (Herford 1929: 10). This personal revelation was of supreme significance for Carpenter. In his writings there does not seem to be a justification for rejecting revelation as applied to persons or events. 'Can a part of history be a *Heilsgeschichte* unless the whole of it is?' (Williams, 1993: 91). It is difficult to determine how personal revelation could be authenticated. What has happened in inter-religious bodies in recent years is that religions have been allowed to speak for themselves, to nurture their own identity, and to look for issues on which to unite that do not impinge on their distinctive doctrinal traditions. Those bodies are far removed from acknowledging a universally recognised, and non-particular, revelation.

Social justice and peace

The participation of British Unitarians in inter-religious bodies in recent years has been more concerned with shared social values than with the development of shared spiritual values. The IARF still has more support from British Unitarians than other inter-religious bodies, because of the similarity of aims between the Unitarian General Assembly and those recently issued by the IARF. For many years now, the Unitarian General Assembly has passed resolutions in favour of social goals. In 2001 the General Assembly opposed the increase in religious foundation schools as being a threat to multi-culturalism (General Assembly, 2001:14). In 2002 it supported the Global Cease-Fire Day and called for an end to Israeli occupation of Palestine (General Assembly, 2003:13-14). These declarations were very much in parallel with the statements issued by the leadership of the IARF (Traer, 1998:2; van Herwijnen, 2000:2; Religious Freedom Young Adult Network, 2003:7).

A significant step was taken in 1997, when the British Unitarian General Assembly joined the World Conference on Religion and Peace, a movement founded in 1970 by several American Unitarian Universalists (Traer, 2000: 6). This seemed to indicate that British Unitarianism had abandoned the hope of uniting the religions into one world faith and had adopted social goals as its focus for inter-religious dialogue. This was further indicated by its joining the Inter-Faith Network for the United Kingdom, an inter-religious body founded in 1987 for the purpose, among others, of working in an environment where there are relationships that 'do not blur or undermine the distinctiveness of different religious traditions' (Inter-Faith Network, 2003:1) and that seek 'to facilitate the fuller participation of the different religious communities in public life' (Inter-Faith Network, undated: 2).

There may still be a hope of convergence of the religions in the minds of some British Unitarians, but it is generally recognised that this is a forlorn hope. In the words of one minister:

> *With hindsight I may realise that, as an inter-faith idealist, I had thought that when we engaged in inter-faith activity, we were doing much more than*

*simply discussing our separate traditions. I saw them as opportunities where
we could begin to see that all paths really led to the same divine goal; that
there was some essential unity of world religions to which our inter-faith
activity gave witness. I now realise that such a view was fundamentally
erroneous.* (Roberts, 2004:5)

The relationships thus established between Unitarians and others have
created an environment for the promotion of social and ethical values. As
will be seen, however, this situation has not sufficed for those Unitarians
who have sought to integrate philosophical or theological elements from
other religions into Unitarianism.

The Dual-Adherence Approach

As a convergence of the religions now seems unlikely, a number of British
Unitarians have taken another approach. Wanting to share in the insights
and practices of other religions has led them to acknowledge allegiance to
two paths: Unitarianism and an apparently contradictory path – an
approach reminiscent of the one taken by John Robinson (1919–1983) in
his book *Truth is Two-Eyed* (1979). Dual Adherence, or even Multiple
Adherence, is an approach that tries to create a transitional stage between
the acknowledgement of one doctrinal system on the one hand and total
absorption of insights from another religion on the other. It recognises
that there are elements in one religion that, at the current stage of
Unitarian development, cannot be fully integrated into Unitarian belief
and practice. It is the product of a situation within contemporary British
Unitarianism that sees a struggle for identity following the current
uncertain position of Liberal Christianity. It is connected with the
distancing of Unitarianism from Christianity that has ensued, both by
positive steps taken within the movement, and by a rejection from
mainstream Christianity.

There are reasons why some British Unitarians have felt it necessary
and acceptable to follow the Dual-Adherence Approach. Although there is
no way of controlling the situation among the laity, anxiety has been
expressed particularly by ministers and lay leaders of congregations. There
are only a few examples, but the trend does represent a phenomenon that
has arisen only in recent years.

Christian rejectionism

Although devotional paths have not been lacking in Christianity, even in liberal Christianity, there have been Unitarians who have sought to express their religion in ways that reject the Christ-focused form of worship and discussion, and seek to develop personal devotional ideas and practices. Such Unitarians find great inspiration in the teachings arising out of India. For example, as already mentioned in Chapter 1, Eric Breeze, currently minister of two Hyde congregations, is a member of the Theosophical Society. There have been Unitarian ministers before him who have held membership of the Theosophical Society. As noted in Chapter 1, George Parkinson, a minister from 1936 to 1980, was a Theosophist for many years while ministering to the Unitarian churches in Scarborough and Whitby. A number of Unitarians in the north-west are also Theosophists, many of them connected with the Lodge that meets in the Unitarian Church in Bank Street, Bolton.

Theosophists often claim that membership of their Society implies no adherence to any particular set of doctrines or religious position. In fact, its own literature makes clear that, for acceptance into membership, an applicant need affirm only the first of its objects (Internet Encyclopedia of Philosophy, 2003: 4). This states that the Society seeks 'to form a nucleus of a Universal Brotherhood of Humanity without distinction of race, colour, sect or creed' (United Lodge of Theosophists, undated [a]: 1). Nonetheless, the Society's literature also makes clear that it has a set of teachings that are a contrast, both to mainstream Christianity and, more specifically, to traditional Bible-based Unitarianism. 'One of the main doctrines taught by Theosophy is that of reincarnation' (United Lodge of Theosophists, undated [b]:1). Helena Blavatsky (1831–1891), who founded the Society in 1875, stressed that her new movement was to be in no way connected with Christianity. 'Christianity is now the religion of arrogance, par excellence, a stepping-stone for ambition, a sinecure for wealth, sham and power' (Blavatsky, undated: 138). Annie Besant (1847–1933), a later leader of the Society, declared the Indian sacred writings to be the foundation of all religion. 'I confined myself to the Hindu Scriptures, and in all cases I stated that I regarded these scriptures and the Hindu religion as the origin of all scriptures and all religions' (Besant, 1894).

Thus, it would seem that a new attitude had appeared within British Unitarianism: that one's inspiration could be drawn principally, not from Christianity, however liberal that may be, but from another world religion. This is supported by Robert Bowler's adherence, while he served as minister of the Cotswold Group of Unitarian Churches, to the religious group known as Sant Mat, Surat Shabd Yoga, or Radha Soami Satsang Beas, a movement seeking to connect the aspirant to 'the primal word or sound current' (Seekers Way, 2003: 2). The Satsang was founded in 1861 by Shri Shiv Dayal Singhji (1818–1878), a performer of miracles who taught belief in a Supreme Being that was superior to God and could be known only by particular saintly individuals (Mathur, 2003: 4). The movement arose out of Hinduism and has sought adherents from various religions. Its culture and its teachings are, nevertheless, closer to Hinduism than to any Western form of religion.

Radical individualism

Some Unitarians have argued that British Unitarianism need not absorb insights from other religions or seek to found a new religion based on the best in all those existing. Instead, they would argue that Unitarianism is an empty vessel, a body without tradition, and a place where, completely free of teachings of the past, they can be free to explore other religions and practise openly what they find. An exemplar of this attitude is Art Lester, now the minister in Croydon. Lester was a follower of Merwan Irani, known as Meher Baba (1894–1969), an Indian teacher who believed himself to be God in human form and an incarnation of many religious leaders and teachers, including Zoroaster, Rama, Krishna, Buddha, Jesus, and Muhammad. 'He is the Christ, the Saviour, the Prophet, the Avatar. He is no less than God Himself, taking human form yet again' (Meher Baba Association, 2003: 5).

That Lester was comfortable within Unitarianism despite his admiration for Meher Baba says something about a trend within modern British Unitarianism. This seeks to suspend Unitarian tradition and look beyond the movement to what society in general appears to be seeking. Lester has identified, in the growth of New Religious Movements, in New Age communities, and in depth psychology, a search for spiritual meaning. For him, the Unitarian movement is a vehicle for one's search where all views are welcomed. He has suggested that Unitarianism is now in a position to 'make and re-make our reality' (2000: 32). Lester's Unitarianism is not about adhering to a religious tradition, but providing space whereby individuals can work on their own salvation by drawing from whichever spiritual teachings speak to their condition.

We must not change to save Unitarianism, because Unitarianism is only a tool. Its value has been as a lens by which to apprehend the holy, not as an institution. (2000: 34)

Included among Lester's searchers would probably be those Unitarians who are also members of the Sathya Sai Baba movement. Sai Baba Unitarians are known to be active in Unitarian congregations in Horsham and Gorton in Manchester. Although the Sai Baba movement arose out of the Hindu tradition, it focuses on five principal universal values of truth, righteousness, peace, universal love, and non-violence. The reason why Sathya Sai Baba appeals to some Unitarians is, at least in part, his acknowledgement of one basic religion based on love.

There is only one religion, the religion of love. There is only one language, the language of the heart. There is only one race, the race of humanity. There is only one God, and He is omnipresent. (Sathya Sai Baba, 2003: 3)

Also included in the 'radical individualist' category are those Unitarians who have declared themselves Buddhists, or to be practitioners of Buddhist devotional techniques. Since the late nineteenth century there have been many British Unitarian admirers of Buddhism. Scholars such as Estlin Carpenter, though critical of Buddhism, were nonetheless convinced of the nobility of Buddhism and its ethical teachings (1906). Richard Armstrong, too, speaking from a clearly Protestant position, claimed that genuine Buddhism was something beautiful that could be discerned by looking beyond the 'trappings' associated with Buddhist worship and ritual. 'They may add tinsel and gewgaws. But the beautiful original shines brighter than its uncouth trappings' (1870: 184).

The difference between then and now is that British Unitarians are now prepared, either to use Buddhist devotional methods, or to integrate Buddhist ideas into their own theological position. In 1972, for example, the late Rev. John Storey (1935–1997), a former Congregationalist minister who moved to Unitarianism in 1963, founded the Unitarian Buddhist

Society (Hughes, 2000: 108). He was also responsible for writing hymns in praise of the Buddha and his teachings, including 'Homage to thee, Perfect Wisdom' (Knight, 1987: 11), based on the Rahulabhadra of the Mahayana tradition, and 'Religion needs to permeate' (*ibid.*: 189), based on words of the Dalai Lama. More recently, Rev. Christopher Goacher, formerly serving in Liverpool and now working in Derby, became active in the Community of Interbeing, a Zen Buddhist body that follows the teachings of Thich Nhat Hanh, a Vietnamese monk now living in France. Goacher was also instrumental in founding a Unitarian Buddhist Group in the Liverpool Church where he was minister for several years (Goacher, 2004: 44). Also, Jane Barraclough, the minister to the Bethnal Green congregation in London, has acknowledged that she is a regular practitioner of Buddhist devotion (Barraclough, 2003: 3), and that she understands the world 'largely mediated through a Buddhist lens' (Barraclough,2004: 13-14), although she is agnostic about Buddhist cosmologies (p. 14). Furthermore, Mark Shiels, a Unitarian minister living in Bath, operates a 'Buddhist and Contemplative psychospiritual approach to psychotherapy' (Shiels, 2004:1).

Perhaps the reason why some forms of Buddhism are attractive to Unitarians, and why they have felt able to combine adherence to the two traditions, is that such bodies often claim to be unclosed systems of belief, as merely partial discoveries of a greater truth yet to be discerned. Thich Nhat Hanh has said himself, as part of his Fourteen Precepts, that there is no absolute truth, and that no knowledge is changeless.

> *Do not be idolatrous about or bound to any doctrine, theory, or ideology,*
> *even Buddhist ones. All systems of thought are guiding means; they are not*
> *absolute truth.* (2003: 4)

This viewpoint is not unlike the traditional position within Unitarianism: that religious doctrines, even Christian ones, are mutable. 'Again, the doctrines that have been connected with Christianity, and taught in its name, are quite as changeable as the form' (Parker, 1864: 7). Estlin Carpenter expressed the same attitude in a more poetic way:

> *The earthen vessels enshrining the treasure are shattered in the light of*
> *modern knowledge, and the treasure itself turns out to be something different*
> *from what was first supposed.* (1910: 12)

56

British Unitarians could, therefore, claim that participation in a movement that shares with Unitarianism a concept of the transience of religious doctrines is an act consistent with Unitarian values and principles.

It could be claimed that radical individualism has its limits. In recent years a controversy developed that tested the limits of tolerance and raised the question of whether individual freedom within Unitarianism could be stretched to movements that had structures parallel to those of Unitarianism but whose approach to religious discovery was diametrically opposed. A senior minister with some years' experience declared himself an adherent of an African movement known as the Brotherhood of the Cross and Star. Dr Jeremy Goring, an academic and former Dean of Goldsmiths College, London, was also Honorary Minister of Westgate Unitarian Chapel, Lewes. In 1991 he joined the Brotherhood of the Cross and Star, and ultimately was consecrated bishop and European Representative. Still retaining his Unitarian affiliation, and still ministering to the Unitarian congregation in Lewes, he was subjected to a new policy of the Unitarian General Assembly that deleted the names of anyone from the accredited Roll of Ministers who held a leadership position in another religious movement.

Although the Brotherhood claims not to be a church but 'a movement of the spirit embracing not only Christians but also the adherents of other religions' (Brotherhood of the Cross and Star, 2003: 1), it does have clearly enunciated religious doctrines. Its leader, Olumba Olumba Obu, is claimed as a special messenger sent to proclaim the Kingdom of God as a present reality. The Old Testament was recognised as the Age of the Father, and the New Testament as the Age of the Son, while now we live in the Age of the Spirit – represented by Olumba Olumba Obu and members of the Brotherhood (Goring, 2003: 4). Some of the admirers of Obu have made great claims for him: that he is a 'Super-Spiritual Existence' (Inyang-Ibom, 2003: 1) and an incarnation of Jesus Christ (Unity of Nations, 1967: 6). Such views do not sit easily with Unitarianism, although it is difficult to say clearly why such an approach should not be acceptable. It is noticeable, for example, that the Brotherhood's teachings about the person of their leader are not so different from those claimed for the person of Meher Baba, to which Art Lester adheres.

Spiritualism

There is a certain logic to British Unitarians' membership of other religious movements that declare themselves free of dogma. Spiritualism is thus a movement that has acquired support from some Unitarians. This is not such a recent phenomenon as may be assumed. John Page Hopps (1834–1911), a Unitarian minister and hymn writer celebrated for writing the hymn 'Father lead me day by day' (Baxter *et al.*, 1991: 250), was also a spiritualist and was for a while President of the Manchester Spiritualist Society and editor of a spiritualist journal known as *Light* (General Assembly, undated: 4). His views were unusual for the time, however.

There is evidence of a greater interest in spiritualism in more recent times. Following the psychical experiences of Rev. George Whitby (1906–1980) in the early 1960s, the Unitarian Society for Psychical Studies (USPS) was founded in 1965 to study psychical phenomena with a critical and open mind. Since then, however, some Unitarians have found the confidence to urge that the movement should not strive to be so objective but should be willing to engage more affirmatively in psychical or spiritualist experience. The USPS has welcomed into its membership many who would admit to being convinced of the case for spiritualism.

> *I wonder, can the USPS afford to be quite so unrelated to the situation prevailing in our denomination at this time? Can we, as people who are willing to recognise the importance of the psychical element in human nature, be content with such a massive ignorance of this factor in our congregational and denominational life?* (Roberts, 1989a: 5)

In recent years there have been Unitarians who have combined their membership of a Unitarian congregation with membership of a spiritualist organisation. Also, one minister has defined himself as, among other things, a 'free spiritualist' (see Appendix 1). Although there is a small Christian spiritualist denomination, known as the Greater World Christian Spiritualist Association, most spiritualists belong to the Spiritualist National Union. The latter movement is based on seven basic principles that make no mention of Christianity. It claims not to be tied to any creed or dogma (SNU, 2003: 1). Like Unitarianism, spiritualism claims to be a rational religion with a philosophical and scientific approach (Meynell, 2003:1). It is, therefore, no great surprise that some Unitarians could feel at home in such a body.

British Neo-Paganism

Another trend within modern Unitarianism is the adherence of some members, including ministers, to British Paganism. In the survey conducted for the thesis on which this book is based, no fewer than six ministers defined themselves as pagan in some way, although one identified with 'panentheist/creation spirituality', and three others combined their paganism with some other appellation (see Appendix 1). The Unitarian Earth Spirit Network (UESN), founded in the 1990s as the Unitarian Neo-Pagan Network, although now omitting the word 'pagan' from its title, nonetheless defines itself as a body 'affirming a Pagan spiritual perspective' (Mitchell, 2000: back page). It has more than 130 members, of whom 22 are Unitarian ministers, including the current Principal of the Unitarian College, Manchester and two former Presidents of the Unitarian General Assembly. Among its membership there are, as well as many who have not defined their relationship with paganism, several members of the Wicca movement, two ministers who are also members of the Order of Bards, Ovates and Druids, and at least one shaman (Mitchell, 2003: unpaginated). One member, Cynthia Dickinson, served for a while as the Vice-President and a National Committee member of the Pagan Federation, an organisation that has attracted several UESN members and openly acknowledged British Unitarianism as embracing Paganism (Pagan Federation, 2001: 6). The congregation where Cynthia Dickinson defines her Unitarianism – Westgate Chapel, Wakefield, where pagan rituals are held regularly – is also the home congregation of a lay Unitarian who served for a while as Pagan Visiting Minister to Wakefield Prison.

At this point it is necessary to ask why elements of British Unitarianism have embraced paganism. The answer lies in several milestones of British Unitarian history. Firstly, a number of events took place in 1981 that gave evidence of a new interest in women's spirituality and feminist theology. The Women's Group of the Golders Green congregation produced a number of services of worship using material that celebrated the feminist reconstruction of pre-Christian nature religions, such as that found in Starhawk's *Spiral Dance* (1979). In 1981 a new national women's group was formed with a specifically feminist stance that studied, among other topics, spirituality and God and what it meant to be a Unitarian woman (Peart, 1999: 64).

Secondly, in 1985, following a resolution passed in 1982, the General Assembly published the report of a working party that was set up to consider the implications of feminist theology for the life of the Unitarian movement. This report, to be used by congregational discussion groups, promoted the idea, among others, of using female imagery for the divine in worship and in Unitarian teachings. The principle to be adopted, according to its convenor, was to place personal experience above the views of 'experts' (Croft, 1984: 1). The report stressed the need to rethink theology by allowing for a reclamation of the possibility of God's being envisioned in the feminine.

Thirdly, the American Unitarian Universalists witnessed the creation, in 1986, of the Covenant of Unitarian Universalist Pagans, a body that sought to be an earth-centred focus within Unitarian Universalism and a gateway to UU paganism for the larger Pagan community (Burwasser, 1996: 4). One of the most celebrated Unitarian Universalist Pagans is Margot Adler, a prominent witch and author of *Drawing Down the Moon* (1979), the most celebrated book on American Neo-Paganism. Her adherence to both Wicca and Unitarian Universalism is due to her need for a balance that allows for her exploration of rationalism alongside her pursuit of joy within earth-centred spirituality. The mixture of the two traditions brought, she affirmed, a greater joyousness in ceremony, a more creative and artistic ability, a richer liturgy, and 'a bit more juice and mystery' (Adler, 1996: 7). This new organisation quickly increased in membership and was an inspiration for the creation, by Rev. Peter Roberts, of the British body, the Unitarian Earth Spirit Network.

Fourthly, the global ecological crisis diverted the attention of many Unitarians, who sought a way to deal with the problems of the environment by rethinking the Unitarian theological position. The traditional concept of God as Creator was challenged by a growing belief in humankind as co-creators with God. Increased emphasis on ecological themes became more evident in hymns, prayers, and sermons; for example, the hymn 'Stranger on the Mountain' refers to a 'stranger' who 'spoils the ancient meadow, laying waste the forest green' (Knight, 1987:207). Unitarians began openly to consider pantheism as a viable theological position. Dr Rosemary Griffith, a lay theologian now known as Rosemary Arthur, has suggested that only pantheism may lead to a true concern for the world. 'Once we realise that all matter is divine, that all living things are divine, then (and only then) will we respect them' (1994: 6). Neo-Paganism, then, has become a viable form of religion for a number of British Unitarians seeking to live out traditional Unitarian principles.

Conclusion

British Unitarianism has demonstrated different ways of responding to the challenges of inter-religious dialogue. So far, however, little has been said in this book about the impact of those responses on the actual practice of British Unitarianism. In Chapter 4 this aspect will be addressed by considering inter-faith activity in practical terms: Sunday Worship, Occasional Services, and World Religions in Religious Education. Such elements of British Unitarian life may indicate whether or not the British Unitarian movement can still claim to be primarily a Christian denomination, or whether it should now define itself as a universalist or syncretistic faith.

4 The practice of pan-religionism

The previous chapter examined the contribution of British Unitarians to inter-religious dialogue. This chapter goes on to consider how the dialogue with other religions, and the absorption of elements of other religions into Unitarianism, have influenced the way in which Unitarianism is practised. It examines first the current Unitarian practices within the inter-faith movement. It then deals with ways in which Unitarian Sunday worship has changed in general to meet those new insights from other religions. Then follows a consideration of the changes to occasional services. Some reference will then be made to the altered emphases in religious education.

Inter-religious activity

This chapter will consider the degree to which the beliefs and practices of other religions have impinged upon British Unitarian worship. Such changes have led a number of Unitarians to rethink their relationships with the adherents of other religions. When elements of the sacred literature of another religion have become integral parts of Unitarian worship, one is entitled to ask what kind of relationship with other believers is being practised. Such questions concern, for example, the nature of Unitarian worship itself, and whether it can satisfy the needs of other believers. There is also the question of whether knowledge of other religions leads Unitarians to a closer dialogue with other believers, or whether Unitarians have lapsed into a certain self-satisfaction, believing that they have acquired a universal way and wisdom through the insights accumulated from so many different sources. To answer such questions it is necessary to reflect on the approach to inter-religious activity by modern British Unitarians. Unlike the previous chapter, however, this section reflects on these issues from a practical, rather than a theoretical, position.

Ministerial involvement in inter-faith activity

The number of ministers and lay leaders, consulted in the survey, who reported membership of inter-faith organisations was very high. No fewer than thirty claimed membership of the International Association for Religious Freedom (IARF), with many ministers being involved also in various local inter-faith groups. As many as 32 ministers stated that they held office in an inter-faith organisation, twelve of those at national or international level. Rev. Jopie Boeke, for example, served as President of the International Association of Liberal Religious Women, while Rev. Celia Midgley served as its Secretary for six years. Rev. Dr. Richard Boeke is Secretary of the World Congress of Faiths, and Rev. Feargus O'Connor serves on its national committee. Unitarians currently hold all the officer positions in the British Chapter of the International Association for Religious Freedom, its Chair for many years being Rev. Geoffrey Usher, an officer also of Sheffield Interfaith who has, in addition, worked with the Inter Faith Network. British Unitarians are thus at least as active in inter-faith work as ever before. Geoffrey Usher has gone so far as to declare that inter-faith work is one of the primary duties of a British Unitarian minister (Usher, 2000: 5).

In terms of inter-faith activity, British Unitarian ministers now direct their energies, according to the survey, principally towards meeting adherents of other religions on their own ground, either by attending social functions organised by leaders of other religions or by attending places of worship (see Appendix 1). Nevertheless, there is a good deal of activity taking place on what may be referred to as social or political issues. As a catalyst, the IARF is currently developing a declaration of religious responsibility that seeks to commit its associated membership to promote human rights within their own organisations (Clark, 2003: 2-3). One Unitarian minister sees the role of Unitarianism as being a means of ensuring that the inter-faith enterprise seeks peace and justice as prime reasons for its existence.

We can be happy that our Unitarian contribution to the World Congress of Faiths and the wider interfaith witness for the creation of a global ethic of peace and justice will continue to be much valued in the years ahead. (O'Connor, 2004: 27)

Another major involvement of Unitarian ministers is in attendance at, or participation in, all-faith services. No fewer than 37 ministers in the survey claimed attendance at such events (see Appendix 1). An American Unitarian Universalist publication, providing prayers for inter-faith gatherings (Foerster, 2003), has been made widely available for British Unitarians, but the British Unitarian movement is now providing resources of its own to cater specifically for inter-faith worship. Such material, written to appeal to an inter-faith worshipping community, includes 'Prayer for an Interfaith Service' by Rev. Andrew Hill (2004:15) and my own 'Prayer Based on Words by Guru Arjan' (Marshall, 2004d: 18-19) and the 'Prayer to the Unknown God' (Marshall, 2004c: 35). It seems the British Unitarian movement now sees itself as a tool for the creation of worshipping initiatives, bringing together adherents from different faith traditions. This is important, because inter-faith worship is a sensitive area, avoided by many other groups involved in dialogue. There are difficulties in determining what 'inter-faith worship' actually means: whether it is 'serial worship', in other words a sequence of items presented by different religious representatives from their own traditions, or whether it is something newly produced to satisfy everyone. For some this means that the nature of the British Unitarian movement has changed, in that it is not representative of a particular faith tradition but is in itself an inter-faith body in its own right.

There is a parallel here in the debates of another religious movement claiming freedom from credal statements. Within the Religious Society of Friends is a body of opinion seeking to promote the idea of British Quakerism as a vehicle for the creation of an inter-faith community (Tennyson, 1992; Nesbitt, 2003). The difference between the Society of Friends and the Unitarian movement, however, is the latter's long tradition of organised worship – something eschewed by the Quakers. The Unitarian movement, with its innovative use of material from non-Christian sources, thus has something of an advantage.

British Unitarianism as an inter-faith body

What is new in many Unitarian congregations is a specific and conscious decision to be the spiritual centre for an inter-faith community, a decision that Unitarianism should see itself as that inter-faith community, and that its resources should be directed towards the creation of ventures inclusive of people of different religious traditions. Thus, a number of ministers have declared themselves available to conduct inter-faith weddings and funerals (Silk, 2004: 24; also see Appendix 1). Some have considered themselves as inter-faith ministers, being able to speak to different constituencies in different religious languages as the need arises (Simons, 1983: 21-4). The British Unitarian movement itself has been described as an inter-faith movement. 'In my opinion, Unitarianism is in its very nature an interfaith movement' (Silk, 2004: 23). This is the opinion of one minister who, in a discussion with a Jewish rabbi who identified with thousands of years of Jewish history, declared himself as identifying with the entire human tradition, 'which is much older!' (*ibid.*).

The problems encountered in defining British Unitarianism as an inter-faith movement are various. First, such a definition implies that individual Unitarians can define themselves in terms of one of the great religions of the world. It is true that there is now a vast array of different faith traditions within Unitarianism itself, 'with a spectrum extending from liberal Christianity through to religious humanism' (Hill, 1994: 5). There are still many Unitarians who identify themselves as Christians, and other Unitarians who identify themselves in terms of one other major religion. What is also true, however, is that for many Unitarians the insights from other religions are vast resources to be drawn on, rather than whole packages with which to be clearly identified. For some Unitarians, they are, individually, inter-faith entities within themselves. Furthermore, the radical position within Unitarianism has sought not to identify with the various religious traditions individually, but to identify common values and elements of belief that all could share. This 'universalism' would be, then, something other than the doctrine-based positions of most world religions. This was the vision of Ralph Waldo Emerson, who wrote a poem called 'Blight', lamenting the alienation from the natural world that was a feature of the modern era, which he contrasted with earlier times.

(They) were unitarians of the united world,
And, wheresoever their clear eye-beams fell,
They caught the footsteps of the SAME.
(Emerson, 1899)

A second reason why identifying British Unitarianism as an inter-faith movement is problematic is that all the faith traditions would not be fully represented, and those that were represented would be utilised in a distinctly Westernised way. This is indicated, for example, in the way in which material from the world's religions has been presented in a Christian liturgical style (for example, Hayes, 1954). Some religions are more favoured in Unitarianism than others, the religion of Buddhism, for example, receiving the same kind of welcome today (Barraclough, 2003 & 2004) as it did in the past (Armstrong, 1870). As we saw in the previous chapter, some Unitarians had even created a Buddhist Society within Unitarianism. For some religions, however, there has been a much colder welcome. Although an initiative by the General Assembly in 1992 brought together Unitarians and Muslims in a 'colloquium' (Marshall, 1999: 54), there has been little interest in Muslim insights, with the exception of the work of Jalal al-Din Rumi (1207–1273) and the Sufi tradition, the followers of which tradition have established a dialogue with the Religious Education Department. It is interesting to note that the latest publication on worship resources (Buckle, 1999), as well as using Christian sources, offered material from Native American sources (*ibid.*: 3 & 6), Jewish sources (p. 4), Hindu sources (p. 4), and Buddhist sources (p. 7) but nothing specifically from Islamic sources except a few prayers from *Every Nation Kneeling* (Hayes, 1954). From the newer religions, Unitarianism has had very little input and has indeed displayed some antagonism towards them (Chryssides, 1999: 92). It appears that Unitarians are less attracted to religions that are more insistent upon retaining an exclusive hold on what they consider as the truth.

A third problem with the identification of British Unitarianism as an inter-faith movement is that the structures of Unitarianism are such that they do not convey the impression that, in practical terms, elements of different faith traditions are evident. The way that the Unitarian movement lives and works still bears Christian characteristics. For example, most congregations are gathered in 'churches' or 'chapels', are served by 'ministers' and 'preachers', and worship on the day associated by mainstream churches with Christ's Resurrection. Most of its ministers are trained in Christian ecumenical environments, and many congregations, but not by any means all of them, still participate in local Councils of Churches. Unlike organisations such as the International Association for Religious Freedom, there are no clearly identifiable representatives of other faith traditions. Unlike the World Congress of Faiths, there is an acceptance of the primacy of one particular faith, that of Christianity, as evidenced by the Objects of the General Assembly with its commitment to 'the upholding of the Liberal Christian tradition' (General Assembly, 2002:7). It would be difficult, holding such a position, for British Unitarianism to claim to be an inter-faith movement in itself. If it cannot do so, then, it is necessary to consider the nature of Unitarian's inter-religious work and what place it can have in the life of the movement.

Criticism of Unitarianism's inter-religious activity

It is true that British Unitarians have made, and still do make, a generous contribution to the work of inter-faith organisations. It has to be said, however, that there are Unitarians who have questioned such a contribution. The former Information Officer of the General Assembly has asserted that one of the major purposes of inter-faith activity is dialogue (M.F. Smith, 1996: 3). It is this aspect of the work that has been brought into question. Peter Roberts has claimed that serious dialogue is not what happens at inter-faith gatherings.

> *What happens at most interfaith gatherings is that individuals who belong to some vaguely liberal wings of various faith traditions enter into discussion with each other...but it may appear to outsiders to be a serious dialogue.* (Roberts, 2004: 7)

Roberts then declared that inter-faith activity could not lead to two of the goals shared by many Unitarians: that of a single global religion, or that of a unity of purpose for the world religions (*ibid.*: 8). Roberts is not a Christian Unitarian and does not seek to retain liberal Christianity within Unitarianism, but he does believe that there are aspects of world religions that can hinder the progress that Unitarianism is making in its own spiritual understanding. There is also the issue of whether an inadequate engagement with other religions has led to confusion over the very role of ministry. In an earlier essay, Roberts has suggested that the inadequate understanding of British Unitarianism's faith position, in terms of its stance towards other world religions, has meant that the minister has no real certainty about the role to be played in Unitarian communities.

> *What we do stems from what we are, and this is the question that must be resolved. Shaman? Priest? Scriptural Interpreter? Amateur social worker? College-trained preacher? What next?* (Roberts, 1989b: 30)

A former President of the General Assembly has criticised modern British Unitarianism for not being sufficiently engaged in the area of inter-faith dialogue. Alan Ruston claimed that British Unitarians have been, and still are, limited in their knowledge and understanding of what it means to be a member of a minority faith in Britain. Meetings with other believers have been fleeting, with very little exploration of what a particular religion has involved. Also, Unitarians have tended to view the world faiths as an amorphous whole (Ruston, 2004: 12). Furthermore, he said, there has been insufficient critical exploration of what it means for a theological encounter to take place between Unitarianism and another major religion. This theology of 'interfaithery', he has suggested, is in serious need of development (p. 13).

As can be seen, then, the impact of inter-faith activity upon British Unitarianism has been notable in several ways. Unitarians have adapted the content of their worship to include material from other sources. Services involving participants from different faith traditions have become common. More and more ministers and laypeople have become involved in the whole inter-faith enterprise. The positive consequences of this have been challenged, however, in that the question still remains to be answered: how has Unitarianism changed and developed because of it? The extent of the change and the theological character of modern British Unitarianism are issues to be explored in the concluding chapter.

Pan-religionism and Sunday worship

Unitarian Sunday worship in the nineteenth century

Several features characterised Sunday worship in most Unitarian churches in the nineteenth century, since the creation of the British and Foreign Unitarian Association in 1825. Firstly, as compared with Unitarian worship today, there was a noticeable degree of conservatism. Unlike most of the Free Churches, the use of a service book, complete with responses, canticles, and psalms, was common. The first church to have used the name 'Unitarian', in London's Essex Street, devised its form of worship specifically based upon the Church of England's Book of Common Prayer. This first Unitarian chapel was meant to be 'a rational model of an Anglican place of worship, with a reformed Anglican liturgy' (Short, 1968: 228). It is thus not surprising that Unitarian worship had an Anglican feel about it. This continued to be the case, as witnessed by the numerous Unitarian liturgies written throughout this period. The 1883 edition of the *Unitarian Almanack* recorded no fewer than 25 different liturgies in use, together with a number of others written specifically for individual congregations (BFUA, 1883). According to d'Alviella, however, many of them simply excluded from the Anglican liturgy 'all that possessed a Trinitarian or dogmatic significance', on the grounds that they 'might be acceptable to orthodox congregations in a state of transition' (1886: 91). It is to be noted that, of the 123 traceable liturgies produced by the Unitarian tradition up to 1946, 89 were based on the Church of England's own service book (McGuffie, 1982: 5).

The two most widely used service books, *Ten Services of Public Prayer* (Martineau, 1879) and *A Book of Prayer in Thirty Orders of Worship* (Crompton Jones, 1898), were fiercely conservative, with the exception that direct references to prayer through Jesus Christ were omitted. Two particularly notable editions were those produced by the congregations in Birmingham (1830) and Leeds (1892), which were barely distinguishable from the Book of Common Prayer. Even those congregations not using a service book as such nevertheless filled out their services with responses, chants, and psalms that were all based upon Biblical material drawn from the Anglican tradition. Even into the next century such material was still in use, with books of chants and psalms being prepared by congregations such as Wakefield (1904) and Liverpool (1930).

There was little sign that Unitarian congregations generally were using material from non-Christian sources. Even Estlin Carpenter, the man responsible to a large degree for the familiarisation of the Unitarian movement with the sacred literature of other religions, produced worship material that was of a conservative nature, as in the book of his prayers published after his death (Davis, 1927). There were some important exceptions, however. D'Alviella noted that the congregations in Glasgow, Preston, and Clerkenwell often replaced readings from the Christian scriptures with selections from 'the sacred literature of all ages and (1886: 92). John Page Hopps (1834–1911) was also providing material from non-Christian sources (Hill, 1994: 33), as was Moncure Daniel Conway (1832–1907). Conway was an eminent American Unitarian minister, a member of the Free Religious Association, who worked for a while in Britain. He produced a collection of material for worship from the great religions of the world, entitled *The Sacred Anthology; A Book of Ethical Scriptures* (1876).

The second major characteristic of nineteenth century Unitarian worship is the resistance to innovation. Some of the churches that were new causes in the Victorian period began the practice of open congregational discussion, directly after the service, on the subject of the preacher's sermon. This was a rare occurrence, however, and the practice soon diminished (d'Alviella, 1886: 92). It is true that Martineau influenced the more aesthetically inclined form of worship, with robed choirs, processions, and the building of new chapels that were impressive mock Gothic structures. Nonetheless, this movement tended to be an embracing of elements found in the more conservative churches of the Christian religion. There was no great use of material from non-Christian sources. It is true that hymns were written calling for the establishment of a new universal religion; based on elements from the world's religious heritage, they were written by the Transcendentalist writers of the American Unitarian Association, such as Samuel Longfellow (1819–1892) and Samuel Johnson (1822–1882). These hymns were included in the books used in Britain (BFUA, 1902 and BFUA, 1905), but they did not make specific references to the faith or practices of other religions. It is interesting to note that the hymn by George Matheson (1842–1906), *Gather Us In*, a hymn well used by modern Unitarians for its call to 'gather our rival faiths within thy fold' (Baxter, 1991: 217), was not included in the Unitarian hymn books of the Victorian period or immediately afterwards.

The third characteristic of Unitarian Sunday worship in the nineteenth century was its emphasis on the rational. At least that was the case until the influence of Martineau became so overwhelming. The use of non-Christian material would not have been possible in an environment that was so deeply uncomfortable with anything that appealed to the senses rather than to the rational mind. Harry Lismer Short (1906–1975) described how Martineau had become critical of the rationalist hymns of the day, described by Martineau as 'rhymed theology, versified precepts, or biblical descriptions capable of being sung' (Short, 1968: 258). Martineau wanted hymns to bear emotional content, without too much theological accuracy. Imagination and grandeur were sufficient if they gave merely a general impression of what was believed to be the truth. It was some time, however, before Martineau's comprehensive and inclusive approach became widespread. As late as 1964, the section of the report of the Commission on Unitarian Faith and Action in the Modern World known as 'The Unitarian Churches in Society Today' noted that public worship was still often dominated by reason, and that 'there are many areas of worship where there is room for development' (Kenworthy, 1964: 4).

Unitarian Sunday worship in the twentieth and twenty-first centuries

After the World's Parliament of Religions in 1893, and the establishment of what became known as the International Association for Religious Freedom in 1900, Unitarian Sunday worship gradually became more open to the use of non-Christian literature. This was a slow development, however, as the conservatism within the movement, regarding practice rather than philosophy or actual theology, hindered it from being as innovative as it could have been. The elements within the Sunday service must be analysed, however, to discover where Unitarianism began to display any evidence of being influenced by the world's great religions.

The first element to consider is the structure of Sunday worship. The British Unitarian movement had always displayed a love for order and, although liturgical worship was never universal, a book of liturgical worship – *Orders of Worship* – was one of the first books to be published by the General Assembly, a few years after its establishment in 1928 (General Assembly, 1932a). The services within the book, however, were based exclusively upon material from Martineau's creations and the two service books from the nineteenth century already mentioned. The reluctance to change the structure is exemplified by a publication that appeared in the same year as *Orders of Worship*. In *Prayer: Its Method and Justification*, the writer emphatically asserted the importance of conservatism in worship: 'Old, tested, invaluable material should never be excluded until every effort has been made to enter into it, to understand it, and to appreciate it'; and 'the [service] book as a whole must be nobly ordered, part being adjusted to part as Reason requires' (Clare, 1932: 52).

This attitude made it very difficult to make innovative use of literature from other faith traditions. For many, *Orders of Worship* (GA, 1932a) was acknowledged as a sort of denominational textbook for worship, even though it was not always used as a congregational tool but as a source for the preacher's prayers. As late as 1972 an official publication of the movement was stressing the importance of this resource as an integral piece of literature for lay preachers. 'The best Unitarian publication available is *Orders of Worship* and every lay preacher should possess a copy' (Hosegood, 1972: 7).

As structure within Unitarian worship tended to be difficult to alter, innovations were introduced that managed to use material from other religions while still retaining the formal structure of Sunday worship. Thus, in 1936, Will Hayes produced a service book that was later expanded and published officially by the denominational press (Hayes, 1954). This book had a structure that was very traditional, complete with canticles, formal exhortations, and set hymns. The music recommended for these elements was taken from hymnbooks and music books well used at that time, such as *Hymns Ancient and Modern* (W. H. Monk, 1916). The content of Hayes' services, however, was very different. The words for the canticles, using traditional Christian hymn music, were drawn from the Dhammapada (Hayes, 1954: 25), the words of Lao-Tse (26), and the Bhagavad-Gita (109). Meditations and prayers were taken from the Vedas (25), the Zend-Avesta (27), the Qur'an (27), the Hymn to Amon (27), and the Pancha-Tantra (95). The fact that the denominational press published it indicates the general recognition given to the need for a wider collection of material from which to draw. On the other hand, the formal structure of worship within this book was still traditional.

The publication of service books in the twentieth century was very rare in British Unitarianism. One major exception, however, was the *Unitarian Orders of Worship*. Again, a formal structure formed the basis of liturgical Sunday services that included material from various sources. In Service Six, almost all the material included was taken from non-Christian literature, with prayers and readings from Hindu, Jewish, Buddhist, and Native American sources (Godfrey, 1976: 29-34).

The use of formal structures did create a context that was congenial to the Unitarian traditions of reason and order. There was a dislike of extemporary practice in worship, and formality was believed to create the correct 'atmosphere' (Elliott, 1994: 47). This did impede the movement's exploration of ways of worship that could make full use of non-Christian traditions. However, as we shall see, there have been innovations, in accordance with the Unitarian tradition of allowing for constant change and growth. 'Unitarian worship evolves and adapts, sometimes drastically and frequently and sometimes so slowly you would hardly notice' (Hill, 1994: 19).

The second element to consider is how Unitarian churches have developed a more inclusive use of the content of their Sunday services, in response to the relationships with the literature of other religions. It is very common to have at least one reading from the sacred literature of another world religion (Chryssides, 1998: 55). It is assumed that preachers will wish to use such material, and the denomination's publication of recommended resources reflects this, with its inclusion of books of prayers from Jewish and Hindu sources (Buckle, 1999). A new book of worship material, published by the Provincial Assembly of Lancashire and Cheshire in 2004, includes numerous prayers and affirmations that, though original, draw specifically on non-Christian traditions. There is, for example, an affirmation that positively seeks to create a spiritual system drawing on non-Christian as well as Christian traditions. 'Let our religion look back to the sages of yesteryear, to Gautama, to Muhammad, to Confucius, to Ashoka, to Nanak, to Paul, to the Indian poets, to the Jewish prophets, to the Christian saints' (Marshall, 2004c: 12). A number of preachers now use two major books published by the American Unitarian Universalist Association that include a very large selection of material from non-Christian sources (UUA, 1979 and 1993). One congregation has a special interest in liberation theology and uses material drawn from those minority groups within a number of religions seeking the liberation of the oppressed.

The Hyde Unitarian Fellowship hears about Dallits, Minjung, Black Americans and Africans, First Nation peoples, third world feminist theologians, Islamic liberation theology, and we see some of their material in worship. (Parker, 2003: 7)

It is in the use of hymns that the non-Christian content of Unitarian worship is often most apparent. In modern hymnbooks, British Unitarians have a number of hymns celebrating the diverse religious traditions of the world. *Hymns for Living* (Knight, 1987), for example, the British General Assembly's most recent major hymnal, includes material exulting in the different religious expressions, some of which celebrate a universal revelation (p. 119). In the words of one modern hymn alone, the insights of no fewer than eleven different religious traditions are mentioned (p. 131). New material is constantly being produced that suggests a sharing with other religions in celebrating their feasts. Rev. Andrew Hill, Minister of the

Unitarian congregation in Edinburgh, has, for example, written several hymns that celebrate the festivals of other religions. These include *Let Us Welcome*, a hymn that welcomes the Jewish feast of Channukah together with the Pagan Yuletide, and the Christian Christmas, seeing within them a common theme. Similarly, *Carol of the Heart* parallels the nativity stories of Jesus with those of the Buddha and of Confucius (Appendix 2).

How Sunday worship has changed

At this juncture it is important to ask just how far Sunday worship has changed in British Unitarian congregations to reflect the growing interest in world religions – and whether the changes are substantial and radically affect the direction in which the movement is moving, or whether they are merely an expansion of the resources available for worship.

The first point to note is that there is now a much wider choice of material available for prayers, and, more significantly, for readings. There tends to be little change in the structure of the services in order to benefit from the experience of other religions. Nevertheless, the use of the literature from other religions is now widespread. A publicity leaflet from the Cambridge Unitarian Church, for example, makes this quite clear: 'Unitarian church services may include texts and readings from any one of the world's religious writings' (Cambridge Unitarian Church, undated and unpaginated). The Golders Green Unitarian congregation made a similar claim: 'Golders Green Unitarians' services ...feature readings, hymns, prayers, meditations and inspiration from many diverse religious and cultural sources' (Golders Green Unitarians, 2003: 8).

It is not accidental that insights from other religions have been absorbed by Unitarianism in this particular packaged way. What is of particular interest is the way whereby the movement has positively sought to make use of such material. One minister has made it quite clear that he does not want a change in the practice of Unitarianism but he does want to make use of the sacred literature of the world's religions. 'Gradually I realised that what I was seeking was not in the practices of the religions but in their scriptures' (Walder, 2004: 4). There have been experiments in Unitarian worship and, according to the survey, 37 Unitarian ministers have claimed to conduct inter-faith services (see Appendix 1). These often involve only a selection of material from the sacred literature of other religions, but they do sometimes involve participation by representatives of other religions (Golders Green Unitarians, 2003: 3). It is also to be noted that experiments in worship styles have constantly been explored, some of them being quite radical and seeking to find inspiration in the Pagan tradition (Peart, 1999: 64). Such innovations are as yet at a very early stage, and thus Unitarian Sunday worship, despite its diverse content, is usually, in terms of structure, rather traditional.

The second point to note about Unitarian Sunday worship is that the material drawn from other religions tends to be filtered through a Western interpretation. For example, the popular book *Every Nation Kneeling* (Hayes, 1954) uses Buddhist material that is very Westernised and congenial to the Western worshipper. Thus, there are extracts from *The Light of Asia*, an original Indian Buddhist poem which, when written, caused controversy among Buddhists for its European misrepresentation of the doctrines of *nirvana*, *dharma*, and *karma* (Arnold, 1908: x). Similarly, an anthology of material used by Unitarians for many years, and recommended in the denomination's official list of worship resources (Buckle, 1999: 8), uses translations by Western writers of Hindu and Buddhist classics (Gollancz, 1950: 563). It is true that most translations into English have been the work of Western scholars. In the twentieth century, however, Eastern scholars themselves adequately translated Eastern texts into English. Radhakrishnan's translation of *The Dhammapada* (1950), for example, is the product of a scholarship that bridges East and West but retains the spirit of the original text. Numerous Penguin Classics have been published that employ Eastern scholars to translate into English the great spiritual classics of India. An example of these is the collection of bhakti *vacanas* that are arranged for public worship (Ramanujan, 1973).

Many Unitarians use the works of Kahlil Gibran (1883–1931) in their services, in the belief that his writings are representative of the religious sentiment of the Middle East. Although Gibran lived for many years in the West, his work has been acknowledged as offering something of the Arabic spirit that is found within the religious writings not only of the Maronite Christianity of his childhood, but also of Islam, the Druze, and Judaism (Wolf, 1974: xx). It is important to note how the sacred writings of other religions are used in Unitarian worship, as no fewer than 71 of the 80 ministers who returned their questionnaires claimed to use them in their services (see Appendix 1).

In many ways, the teachings of the world's religions are filtered through the preaching in Unitarian pulpits. Significantly, the knowledge of those religions that Unitarian ministers and preachers use in their preaching has come from academic study of those traditions, and sometimes from personal study, rather than from the educational services of those religions themselves. This is not to say that there is no value in Unitarian treatments of the teachings of other religions. It does mean, however, that the way in which the material is presented is meant to appeal to a specific constituency: that of the searching Western mind. One serving minister has made this clear by stating that all material within a service is open for debate, that it is to be examined and discussed, that there is to be 'dialogue' with it. She cited the example of a contact, an engineer, who was disenchanted with the current state of organised religion. His influences included Krishnamurti, Taoism, and mystical Christianity. 'This is the kind of person to whom our worship needs to be sensitive' (Kirk, 2002: 91).

The third point to note about changes in Unitarian worship is that the material drawn from the sacred literature of other world religions has tended to be very selective. Thus, the teachings of Buddhism on *nirvana,* and the teachings of Hinduism on *karma* and *samsara,* are generally overlooked, although these two religions are, apart from Judaism, those best known to Unitarian ministers (see Appendix 1). The anthologies of readings from the sacred texts of the world that are most used by Unitarians do not offer readings on those subjects (see Hayes 1954, Godfrey 1976, UUA 1979, 1993). Unitarians have preferred to use material that is less controversial, less foreign to the Western ear, and more likely to convey universal ethical values. This does have coherence, in that the material is used to support the accepted values that draw Unitarians together. What it does not do is convey the complete picture of the fundamentals of the world's great religions. It should be noted, however, that that is not necessarily the justification for the use of material from the sacred literature of the world. British Unitarianism has found its own cultural identity and will use whatever material supports its values. A more interesting state of affairs, however, is to be found in the occasional services, where there are elements of something more adventurous being practised. This will be explored in the following section.

Occasional services

Having discovered significant changes in the content of regular Sunday worship in Unitarian congregations, it is now necessary to consider parallel changes in Unitarian occasional services, such as the rites of passage, communion services, and inductions. These play a distinctive role in promoting the values of Unitarianism, in that they are more likely to be attended by non-members.

Occasional services books since 1928

Until the founding of the General Assembly in 1928, there was no publication that could be considered as in any way an 'official' denominational book of occasional services. Ministers would be required to use their own material, to adapt the resources of other denominations, or, as regards services such as the communion service, to use a book designed specifically for the use of a particular congregation. Notable examples are the Communion Books produced by the congregation of the Old Meeting Church, Birmingham (Thomas, 1912) the High Pavement Chapel, Nottingham (High Pavement Chapel, 1914), and the Service Book used by the Unitarian College, Manchester (McLachlan, 1926).

In 1932, a gap in the provision of resources was filled when the General Assembly produced a companion to its service book (General Assembly, 1932a), *A Book of Occasional Services*, which included the rites of passage together with a communion service (General Assembly, 1932b). This book, however, was not a particularly radical document. Although, unlike its companion book, it did depart quite significantly in structure from its Anglican counterpart, it was nonetheless a Bible-based and conservative publication. The homily for the communion service, for example, made it quite clear that it was to be considered as an office within the Christian tradition. 'We come together to have communion with God through Jesus Christ' (General Assembly, 1932b: 21-2). That the book did not take a radical position is exemplified by the surprising inclusion of a service of thanksgiving after childbirth, to which it referred in brackets as 'Churching' (General Assembly, 1932b: 8).

A new book of occasional services, *In Life and Death*, was published by the denomination 36 years later (Twinn, 1968). This book did make some departures from the style and content featured in the earlier book. Non-

Biblical material was used, though the texts were primarily from classical English poetry, and the communion service was presented as a service of memorial of 'our brother, Jesus, his life and love and unselfishness and power, his teaching and all that he has meant for mankind' (*ibid.*: 82).

Not everyone in the movement used the new book, however. There were ministers who took a more radical position and designed their own material, making use of the sacred writings of other religions. A communion service that I designed myself while ministering in Birmingham, for example, used material from Indian and Jewish sources (Marshall, 1986). A big change came with the publication, in 1993, of a new denominational service book, *Celebrating Life* (Hill, 1993). This was a radical publication in many ways, not least because of its inclusion of services for the end of a marriage (p.91) and the blessing of a same-sex union (p.63). The book also made much use of material from non-Christian sources. Almost every service in the book included such material. The funeral service alone managed to include material from Jewish, Hindu, Buddhist, Zoroastrian, and Native American sources (pp.97ff).

The influence of world religions in current occasional services

The influence of other world religions on occasional services currently used in Unitarian worship can be identified in several ways. Firstly, there have now appeared several new elements in traditional rites, elements that are drawn from other traditions. For example, in the marriage service in *Celebrating Life* (Hill, 1993: 40) the couple drink from a wine cup. This is inspired by the Jewish tradition, and the words used are drawn from the service book of the liberal Jewish tradition (Union of Liberal and Progressive Synagogues, 1967: 421). Also, the service for the scattering of ashes includes an invocation of the elements upon the ashes of the departed, using words drawn from a Brahmin burial service (Hill, 1993: 127). This clearly indicates that the Unitarian movement is able not only to use material from other religions, but also to introduce new elements within its special observances. It is only a tentative step at this stage in the life of the movement, but it must be remembered that this change in approach was a giant step beyond what prevailed previously. Now, it is not merely a repackaging of appropriate words into a traditional context, but an experimental adjustment to a traditional structure.

Secondly, the new book introduced officially the idea of a celebration of a birth that need not involve child baptism. In fact, the book allowed for two very different services, 'The Celebration of a Birth' (Hill, 1993: 69) and 'Christian Baptism' (p.165). For a number of years, some Unitarian ministers had eschewed the concept of child baptism on theological grounds, believing that baptism was a rite within the Christian tradition of which they did not feel a part. Now there was a recognised rite with a distinctly Unitarian character, but one which was influenced by non-Christian sources. The book introduced the idea of the invocation of the spirits of the natural world upon the child, something from the Native American Omaha tradition, although it was not clear in the book how this was to be done (p.74). Nevertheless, the fact that such a departure was made from the norms of the Christian tradition is to be noted. It does suggest a willingness, though it may be tentative and far from universal, to allow for a change, not only in content but also in the character of the rites that Unitarians perform.

Thirdly, the communion service featured in the book has encouraged interest in the partaking of food in a service. At first sight it appears that the communion service was more traditional than the brief services that featured in the earlier books. The name allocated to the service, for example, was 'Christian Thanksgiving' (Hill, 1993:131), a literal translation of the commonly used word 'Eucharist'. The structure of the service was also much closer to that employed by the early church than to any of the previous communion services within British Unitarianism. On closer examination, however, one can see that much of the material was non-Christian (pp.136, 159). There was also a rubric making it clear that different elements and different religious languages could be used. The British Unitarian movement has begun to be more experimental in this regard.

One major American publication that has been influential in the past few years is *The Communion Book* (Seaburg, 1993). There are services therein, such as a Passover Service and two services of Haggadah (pp.321, 329, 352), that are drawn from the Jewish tradition and use the partaking of traditional Jewish foods. There is also a Fire Communion Service (p.189) drawn from the Pagan tradition, which includes elements featured in *The Spiral Dance* (Starhawk, 1979) such as the casting of a circle, the lighting of a flame in the cauldron, and dancing beneath the sky. It should be emphasised that only a minority of British Unitarians enjoys such practices. Nevertheless, it does indicate that there is a tendency to allow change, to experiment and to introduce elements of the devotional practices of other faith traditions. Such innovations within the last few years are very radical and may indicate where the movement is heading.

World religions in religious education

The impact of inter-religious dialogue upon Unitarian religious education programmes for children and adults in the United Kingdom has been varied. The history of organised religious education for children in particular reveals a marked decline since the early twentieth century, when there were numerous resources for Sunday Schools, with a national Sunday School Association producing materials for weekly lessons, and district Sunday School Associations often producing their own pro- grammes and courses. Currently, there are only a few Sunday Schools in existence within the British Unitarian movement. They tend to be more successful in the north of England, particularly in Cheshire and Greater Manchester (where I recently served as President of the North Cheshire Unitarian Sunday School Union). This does indicate a difference between Unitarianism in the north and south of England. Northern Unitarianism tends to be more traditional and has less difficulty in finding resources for religious education, in that it draws on material within mainstream Christianity. Southern Unitarianism tends to be more theologically diverse, and educational resources for such a varied constituency are limited. Because of the scarcity of financial resources at national level, very little in the way of organised programmes is available. Despite that, it is possible to form some idea of the impact of world religions on children's religious education within British Unitarianism.

Religious education for children

At the beginning of the twentieth century, Unitarian Sunday Schools were very active (as in the Free Churches generally). Printed resources were sophisticated and detailed. The content of such programmes, however, was limited to a Biblical understanding of religious faith and practice. The major resource in use at the time was *Monthly Notes for Sunday Classes*, a programme of lessons produced in book form and made available to

Sunday Schools and district organisations. The subjects of the lessons included modern poetry, industry, and culture; but most of the content featured teachings on the Prophets, the Psalms, and the life and work of Jesus. The 1905 edition, for example, focused on eleven psalms, a study of four Old Testament characters, and Bible lessons on subjects such as Faith, Sin, and the Kingdom of God. There was no reference in that publication to the teachings of other world religions (Pritchard, 1905).

The years immediately following the formation of the General Assembly in 1928 saw a well-resourced and efficient Religious Education Department, which considered children's religious education to be a major priority. Separate materials were produced for the different age groups and were issued at regular intervals. Compared with earlier material, the curriculum was noticeably more inclusive, with a separate section of studies referred to as 'Other Faiths'. There were life histories of the great leaders of other religions. There was still, however, an implication that Christianity was the religion against which others were to be compared. In one particular course book, for example, there is an unsympathetic reference to the religion of 'the rude savage' and the suggestion that such a religion attempts to use God for its own purposes, or 'to fashion Him and worship Him in some manner for itself' (Lister, undated: 15).

A remarkable change of direction was evidenced by the publication of Margaret Barr's book, *The Great Unity*. This book contained a programme of course materials that sought specifically to convey the contents of the various religions without holding up one of them as a model, but viewing them all as components of 'the Great Unity of Races and Religions' (Barr, 1937: 9). The book was inspired by Will Hayes (p. 3) and bore some of the characteristics of Hayes' work by focusing, for example, on the major founders of the religions, or the 'Way-Showers' (p. 34), in the belief that children would learn best by identifying with heroes (p. 7). It is difficult to assess, however, how far Margaret Barr's book was used and what its impact was. Its systematic presentation of the founders of the different religions was not copied by later programmes. In fact, a much later programme gave no attention to other world religions at all, and stated that the Unitarian movement was based on the Bible and the teachings of Jesus. 'Our religion and our "inheritance" begin with the Bible. The great movement which is now "our churches" begins with the words of Jesus' (Richards, 1959: 50).

The significant change in young people's religious education came about with a replacement of the systematic approach to teaching – moving from one block of religious teaching to another – by a more thematic style of teaching in education generally at that time. This allowed for teaching from other religions without specific reference to the religion involved, as its doctrines simply blended in with the other material in use. For example, in a lesson on the 'Wonder Part', the seed that gives life to fruit, the story was told of the boy who was asked by his father to break open the seed of a fruit. The boy saw nothing and learned from this that life came out of nothing (Jones, undated-a: 31-2). This story, from the Upanishads (Mascaro, 1965: 117-18), was thus related without any obvious connection to its specific origin. This pattern continued in Unitarian religious education for children.

The present position of children's religious education in British Unitarianism in terms of the impact of other religions can be summarised as follows. Firstly, the predominance of Christianity as the prime religion on which to base religious teaching is now no longer apparent. (There are Sunday Schools still using Biblical teachings, but these are few and they are unsupported by the movement's resources. The two major congregations in Hyde, for example, are untypical of the Sunday Schools within the movement, their renunciation of the title 'Unitarian' being indicative of their closeness to mainstream Christianity.) Secondly, the teaching about other religions has become much more subtle. Their values and beliefs are now being conveyed in such a way that they are considered as integral elements of the Unitarian position, into which they are naturally absorbed in a manner that is congenial to the Unitarian spirit of inclusiveness. Thirdly, there is a sentiment within the movement that elements of the teachings of other religions are taken for granted within religious education, that their inclusion in programmes need not be justified: that what was once considered 'alien' is now essential to Unitarian teaching. For those who are unaware, the elements of the teachings of other religions are barely visible, so far have they become integrated. In adult religious education, however, the impact of other religions has manifested itself in a slightly different way.

Religious education for adults

The first thing to note about adult religious education in British Unitarianism is that it does not have a long history, compared with that for children. The production of written materials has a fairly recent history, with the exception of courses specific to the training of lay preachers. The impact of world religions on British Unitarianism and their influence on adult religious education programmes is best considered with reference to the different stances taken by various initiatives over the last few decades.

The inclusive approach

This approach suggests that there is a clear set of ideas and beliefs that have come into Unitarianism from the religious world beyond Christianity. These ideas and beliefs can be clearly identified and have been formulated into a school of thought designated as 'universalism'. This approach is exemplified by the book *Understanding Unitarians* (Hewett, 1992), which has been used as a basis for adult education sessions in a number of congregations as it is a brief yet challenging attempt to give modern Unitarianism a simple and coherent definition. The writer identified the 'Universalistic' strand as possessing a number of characteristics, many of which have entered into Unitarianism following association with the ideas and beliefs of other religions. These include 'natural religion...inclusive, eclectic or syncretistic approaches ... pantheistic tendencies, mythological polytheism, paganism ... (an) Oriental approach to life, (that is) also present but submerged in the Western tradition' (*ibid.*: 13).

The implication of Hewett's approach is that there are three forms of modern Unitarianism: the Christian, the Humanistic, and the Universalistic. This suggests that the encounter with world religions has made a huge impact upon British Unitarianism, but that it has manifested itself in a clearly defined section of believers within the movement, although that section is in itself quite diverse. The appeal of Hewett's approach is that he was able to define those three strands in terms of interlocking circles. There are thus points of meeting whereby some followers of those three traditions are merged in an intersection of the circles, yet others are within the orbit of one circle but further away from the point of intersection. Such an interpretation leaves a collection of groupings within Unitarianism that are more numerous and more diverse than the definition seems to allow at first sight.

The individualistic approach

This approach defines modern Unitarianism in a different way. It focuses, not on groups of Unitarians characterised by their faith positions, but on the way that the impact of different religious teachings has created a movement of individuals, all with differing religious beliefs. The adult education tradition following this approach encourages individuals to find their own distinct faith position with the aid of the various religious teachings available. The model for this approach is a programme that was originally designed by the American movement but was adapted and redesigned to address British Unitarianism. *Building Your Own Theology: The British Version* (Midgley, 1990), which has been distributed throughout the movement for use in adult education classes, barely identified the teachings of the different religions at all. Although there was some use of Jewish and Pagan material, the programme did not intend to convey the teachings of other religions. Instead, it encouraged individuals on the course to develop their own stance by working towards the writing of an individual 'credo' (*ibid.*: 53). This faith position could have been developed out of whatever religious and other material was relevant to those individuals' lives.

This approach is further exemplified by another programme designed specifically for British Unitarians in their adult education classes. *Ignition* (Jones, undated-b) was a programme that, once again, provided little in the way of the teaching of doctrines but sought to draw out from participants what they themselves could affirm. It claimed that Unitarianism could not be defined in terms of belief but by its fundamental principles of freedom, reason, and tolerance (*ibid.*: 16). Whether one was a Christian or drew upon the ideas and beliefs of other religions was not the issue that defined a person in Unitarian terms. This allowed for beliefs to be adopted from other religions, but the programme itself did not consider what those individual beliefs were.

The individualistic approach is characterised by an insistence upon each individual Unitarian being a sort of *tabula rasa* upon which is drawn a unique faith position derived from that person's life experiences, background, and religious interests. It takes little interest in the different religions *per se*, finding no reason to examine different religious stances. Instead, it waits for the individual to explore his or her faith in whatever forms may emerge. The problem with such an approach is that it takes so much for granted. It assumes a familiarity with other religions and does not address the implications that arise from (for example) acceptance of aspects of eastern religions such as reincarnation, non-dualism, and the non-monotheistic understandings of the Divine. It has no interest in defining modern Unitarianism, only in encouraging individuals to define their own position. This particular approach does not does not give much indication of the impact of world religions on British Unitarianism, as expressed in religious education.

The pragmatic approach

The pragmatic approach recognises that Unitarianism has had a long-standing relationship with the world's great religions and seeks to convey this in its adult education programmes. It seeks to make use of the material drawn from other religions and to acknowledge that modern Unitarians may find meaning in the teachings of religions other than Christianity, without making any judgements about that fact. *The Unitarian Path* (Hill, 1994) has been used for some years as a resource for adult education classes. It is a course that seeks not to promote any particular position, but to convey what is the current reality within our Unitarian congregations, as understood by the writer. The book made three main statements on the subject. Firstly, Unitarianism is open to and tolerant of other faith traditions (p.33). Secondly, Unitarians may revere the sacred writings of the religions other than Christianity in a similar way to the Christian Bible, and Unitarians may thus speak of 'the Bible of the World' (p.33). Thirdly, the founders and leaders of the non-Christian religions may be considered as guides who may aid us in our search for truth but must not prevent us from enjoying our own spiritual experience.

> But for Unitarians these experienced guides will always graciously step aside and allow us the privilege of a direct personal relationship with the divine qualities of being. (p.60)

This pragmatic approach is further exemplified by various educational initiatives that took for granted the reality of religious pluralism within society and sought to discover where, within the various religious traditions, truth and wisdom could be found. In the Padiham congregation, for example, projects lasting several years have involved visits to the places of worship of various religions, evening courses on different spiritualities, and workshops conveying insights from a number of religious schools. The Oldham congregation holds 'Spirituality Days' with teachings on different spiritual systems such as Native American spirituality, Buddhist techniques, and Paganism. The Birmingham congregation held several years of sessions on religious groups that were little known to Unitarians, whose teachings were believed to be of interest to Unitarians in the development of their own faith stance (Marshall, 1999: 54). The week-long Summer Schools run by the Religious Education Department often include elements such as one from its 2002 programme, 'Flowers from the Interfaith Garden', which sought to integrate aspects of the art, music, and other aspects of culture from other traditions into an eclectic personal Unitarian spiritual culture. Also, the training course for aspiring lay preachers includes a compulsory module on World Religions that teaches the student how to use doctrines, sacred literature, and practices of other faiths in developing Unitarian worship (Marshall, 2003).

Conclusion

As can be seen, the existence of other religions has made an impact upon the way in which modern British Unitarianism is practised. In seeking to be inclusive and responsive to the needs and understandings of its constituent membership, British Unitarianism encountered world religions with an openness to new insights, and even an expectation that the movement would change. That British Unitarianism has changed is a fact. But to what extent can the movement still consider itself to be a Christian denomination? This question is to be answered by how the movement defines itself; by how it is defined by other movements, both Christian and non-Christian; and by considerations of culture and history. In its relationship with other religions, there has never been a formal and satisfactory declaration as to whether British Unitarianism has ejected itself from the Christian religion. Only by a careful analysis of recent acts and statements by Unitarians themselves and by representatives of mainstream Christianity can an answer be made to that most difficult of questions: whether Unitarianism is a Christian denomination, whether it is a 'post-Christian' movement, or whether it is a religious movement in its own right. This will be dealt with in my concluding chapter, along with a reflection on how the study has influenced my own pastoral practice as a British Unitarian minister.

5   British Unitarianism and Christianity

Introduction

The previous chapter considered how the dialogue with other religions, and the absorption of elements of other religions into Unitarianism, has influenced the way in which Unitarianism in Britain is practised. This has led inevitably to the question whether, in the light of such extensive developments, British Unitarianism is still a Christian denomination, or whether it is a religion in its own right. This chapter aims to answer that question. It does so firstly by considering discussions within the British Unitarian movement itself and various attempts to define it from within. Secondly, it reflects on the movement's relationships with Christian bodies in Britain, and the definition of Unitarianism from outside the movement. Thirdly, it examines what it is that defines a religion, and how far Unitarianism can call itself a specific religion. It does this by examining the objections that could be made to its classification as a specific religion.

Internal attempts at definition

In attempting a definition of Unitarianism, I am not merely examining the theological positions of individual British Unitarians but considering how the movement as a whole may be defined. It is possible, for example, for Unitarians to define their individual positions unambiguously in non-Christian terms, while at the same time acknowledging that the movement as a whole is basically a Christian denomination. This is the situation with most of the ministers who completed the questionnaire that was administered as part of my research project: they affirmed a non-Christian position, yet stated that the movement was still primarily a liberal Christian denomination (Appendix 1). The research also uncovered a hesitation on the part of Unitarian ministers to define the movement, in the same way as there is a hesitation in defining individual faith positions. For example, although 42 ministers acknowledged British Unitarianism as a primarily liberal Christian denomination, those acknowledging non-Christian definitions offered as alternatives were numerous and, added together, far outweighed those acknowledging liberal Christianity as the orthodoxy of the movement. The ministers also tended to tick more than one box, and, in a number of cases, classified themselves and the movement in contradictory terms. Some, for example, classified themselves as both Liberal Christians *and* non-Christian Theists at the same time! As already noted in Chapter 3, such 'dual adherence' or 'multiple adherence' is not unusual in Eastern cultures, where, for example, Chinese people can be Buddhist, Confucian, and even Taoist, all at the same time. In the West, however, this would be very unusual. The apparent contradictions indicate the difficulty of giving the movement the precise definition that it seeks but which this chapter attempts.

British Unitarian publications

In order to form some understanding of how British Unitarianism defines itself, it is necessary to consider the several publications in recent years that have sought to reflect the thinking of British Unitarianism in current times. *Understanding Unitarians* (Hewett, 1992) was a popular publication because it was a short read, it grappled with the difficulties that were perplexing Unitarians at the time, it was illustrated by helpful diagrams, and its thesis was a simple one. Hewett argued that there were three clearly defined groups within Unitarianism, namely the Christian, Humanistic, and Universalistic groups. Together they were united in what the author called 'liberality'. For him this meant respecting honest differences and being prepared to engage in dialogue with others of different opinions, on the understanding that each person's faith could be enriched by this.

> *It does not preclude taking a firm stand of one's own, but it does preclude the arrogance that assumes that one's own position is necessarily the only right one.* (Hewett, 1992: 4)

Hewett referred to different theological strands intertwining, just as a rope in which strands of different materials are intertwined (p. 22). Hewett's argument avoided the issue of how a precise definition of

Unitarianism was to be made possible. For him, as now for many Unitarians, there was a difference between identities determined by theory and those deducible from practice.

Publications did begin to seek precision, however, with a greater use of the noun 'religion' to define a body of thought and tradition that was distinctly Unitarian. Although Unitarianism had been described as a 'religious movement' for some time (Hostler, 1981: 78), there had never been an inference that Unitarianism was a distinct religion *per se*. In *The Unitarian Path* (Hill, 1994), although the word 'community' was most often used in terms of the Unitarian presence in society (p. 11), the word 'religion' did appear, though without a definite or indefinite article. The reference was simply to 'Unitarian religion' (p. 6), reflecting a hesitation to give even that label a more precise definition. The introduction of the word 'religion', however, did introduce into the debate the suggestion that the movement may be seeking to acknowledge itself as a world faith in its own right.

This search for independence as a religion has featured in a number of essays written by ministers and lay leaders who, though still hesitating to use the word 'religion', nevertheless indicated quite strongly that Unitarianism was a pan-religionist or 'universalist' faith (O'Connor, 2001: 11) which was no longer Christian (McNeile, 1993: 6) but post-Christian (Lovis, 1994). The word 'religion' once more came into its own when the new Objects of the General Assembly were adopted, with 99 per cent approval, in 2001. The first Object sought '*to promote a free and inquiring religion*' (General Assembly, 2002: 7). Did this mean that such a religion was an aspiration towards which to work, or that it was a current reality? The question was dealt with unambiguously by the publication entitled *Building Our Identity* (Gilley, 2002), a religious education programme focused specifically on the new Object. 'Unitarianism is, first and foremost, a *religion*' (the author's emphasis) (p. 11)

It would be surprising if such an argument were to be made without some disagreement. There are still outspoken Unitarians who, over the past thirty years, have affirmed that Unitarianism has every reason to acknowledge itself as a Christian denomination. 'The Unitarian and Free Christian movement is ... a Liberal Christian Church, historically, liturgically, and theologically' (Kennedy, 1987: 3). Kennedy's argument was that the historical tradition, the style of worship, and the choice of material on which to build a worshipping community all indicated a loyalty to the Christian position. He also believed that he had discovered a firm desire among congregations to recover the Christian heritage. Whether or not that is true is difficult to say. What is true is that there are Unitarians who can assert their loyalty to Christianity despite the apparent pan-religionist position affirmed by many.

> *I am still a Unitarian for the same reason that I converted and became a Unitarian; namely my wish to remain in the Christian tradition and to express my loyalty to Jesus Christ as my spiritual leader.* (Bradley, 1995: 4)

An ex-President of the General Assembly, previously for many years the Principal of the Unitarian College, Manchester, expressed similar sentiments. 'But for most of us, the Christ-myth must inevitably remain a part of our cultural inheritance, and I have a feeling that the new Unitarianism will have to be more Christian and not less' (Long, 1978: 15). Long emphasised this view when he affirmed his belief in the need for Unitarianism to adopt a radical Christian agnosticism that 'combines reverence for what is best in the past with an adventurous faith in the future' (Long, 1982: 13). Furthermore, the recent renewed vigour of the Unitarian Christian Association suggests that Unitarian Christianity is alive and well. There are well-attended fringe meetings at the Annual Meetings of the Unitarian General Assembly, and *The Herald,* the journal of the Unitarian Christian Association, now has a wide distribution.

Whether such voices are representative of a larger body of opinion, or whether they are just a few fringe voices denying an inevitable trend can be determined only by looking for other evidence of movement within British Unitarianism.

Internal evidence of movement towards religious independence

One way in which British Unitarianism has appeared to distance itself from its liberal Christian heritage is in the emergence of contemporary groups that represent the diversity of theological opinion. The Unitarian Renewal Group does not promote a particular theology, but encourages a pluralist approach to religion. It makes a distinction between the experiences of life, encapsulated in the term 'religion', and the reflection on experience that can be termed 'theology' (Midgley, 1990: 4). The URG thus seeks to make Unitarianism a meeting ground for the discovery of individuals' own theologies, wherever that may lead. It cannot therefore envisage future Unitarianism as being an integral part of the Christian tradition.

The Unitarian Earth Spirit Network gathers together increasing numbers of Unitarians who are content to seek a Unitarianism that is not monotheistic, that is earth-centred, and that promotes a 'pagan' lifestyle (Mitchell, 2000). Clearly, such a body is enjoying the freedom to practise a religious lifestyle far removed from even a liberal Christian one.

The argument that British Unitarianism is no longer a Christian denomination could be made by reference to the existence of the Unitarian Christian Association. The aim of the Association is, as declared in its journal, 'to preserve and strengthen the Christian tradition within the Unitarian Movement' (Travis, 2004:13). This implies that the Unitarian Christian tradition is no longer the orthodoxy, that it is a dwindling position that needs to be preserved. That a new body had to be created to provide a spiritual home for Unitarian Christians suggests that the British Unitarian movement itself is failing to provide the spiritual support required by Unitarian Christians.

That Unitarian Christianity has been sidelined as just one position among many in Unitarianism is indicated by the way in which traditional Christian hymns were dealt with in the most recent official hymnbook, *Hymns for Living* (Knight, 1987). In that book, which included a great deal of material from numerous non-Christian sources, hymns drawn from the Christian tradition, whatever their content or usage, were compartmentalised into a section entitled 'The Judaeo-Christian Heritage'. This development was recognised by one critic as implying that the movement had 'out-grown Christianity' and was thus Christian only in 'a merely historical sense' (Kennedy, 1987: 3). There is a competing, although privately produced, hymnbook that much more strongly reflects the Christian position. *Hymns of Faith and Freedom* (Baxter *et al.*, 1991) did make something of an impact when it was introduced in 1991; but it was criticised by many for reflecting an outdated piety. *Hymns For Living* is recognised as the official hymnal. It is still in print and in constant use in most British congregations.

Arguments about the status of British Unitarianism still take place within the journals of the movement and via the Internet. Just how far British Unitarianism can refer to itself as a distinct religion, however, is impossible to determine by reference to internal debates alone. There are clues to be found elsewhere in the British movement's relationships with other denominations and Christian bodies.

External definitions of Unitarianism

Major publications

In order to understand how mainstream Christian bodies have sought to define British Unitarianism, it is necessary to note, first of all, what definitions have been attempted in major publications. Inevitably, as with publications within the movement, there has not always been agreement. Also, the way in which others have perceived Unitarianism has altered over time to the same degree that Unitarians have altered their perceptions of themselves. *The Oxford Dictionary of the Christian Church*, for example, was quite unambiguous about Unitarianism as 'a type of Christian thought and religious observance' (Cross, 1957: 1390). *A New Dictionary of Christian Theology*, however, recognised the distance that Unitarianism had travelled from Christianity, by defining it as a 'movement' that 'rejected the uniqueness of Christianity' and acknowledged 'the plurality of divine revelation' (Kent, 1983: 591). Here was a clear statement that, at least in the words of one scholar, Unitarianism, however it chose to define itself, was no longer an integral part of the Christian religion. The *Dictionary of Beliefs and Religions*, in its brief definition of Unitarianism, acknowledged the movement as 'in many ways akin to Christianity' (R. Goring, 1994: 544). If the movement is 'akin' to Christianity, it cannot therefore be a part of it.

The British ecumenical scene

Another means of determining whether or not British Unitarianism is an integral part of the Christian religion is to consider where it fits into the national ecumenical scene. The British General Assembly did participate with the British Council of Churches until the demise of that body in 1992. The General Assembly was an Associate Member of the BCC rather than a full member, its status determined by its inability to affirm the credal statement of faith that formed the basis of the Council. Nevertheless, it participated fully in all the debates and proceedings of the Council. Its position was paralleled by that of the Society of Friends. But in 1992, the

Council of Churches was disbanded in favour of a new body that could attract previously non-participating organisations such as the Roman Catholic Church, a number of 'Black-led' churches, and the Salvation Army. The Council of Churches in Britain and Ireland, later renamed Churches Together in Britain and Ireland (CTBI), decided not to accept the Unitarians' application for full membership but initially recommended Observer status. This application was also rejected, despite strong lobbying, supported by a resolution that was passed overwhelmingly by the Unitarian General Assembly at its Annual Meetings in 1995 (GA, 2004a: 26). Ironically, the CTBI does allow Unitarian representation in its social agencies such as Christian Aid, the Church and Society Forum, and the Racial Justice Network. The resolute refusal of the national ecumenical body to endorse Unitarianism as eligible for any kind of formal membership suggests that mainstream Christianity is more united than ever in its belief that Unitarianism can no longer be recognised as a part of the Christian religion. A further example is the decision in 2006 of the Chester diocese of the Church of England to deny the General Assembly the right, previously allowed, to hold its Anniversary Service in Chester Cathedral.

The situation of the Religious Society of Friends on this issue is interesting. Although its denial of the need for credal statements is akin to that of Unitarianism, the Society of Friends has been accepted into full membership of the CBTI. This has caused some degree of discontent within Quakerism itself, however, and there are still many dissenting voices.

The policy of local ecumenical bodies is less clear than at the national level. Local Councils of Churches, sometimes known as Churches Together, are free to write their own constitutions, and some of them are more welcoming of Unitarian congregations than others. Some Unitarians have played very active parts in such bodies, even becoming office-holders. In other bodies, however, the presence of Unitarians in itself has caused controversy and led to resignations from those churches unable to acknowledge Unitarianism as a Christian community. In two towns in Greater Manchester, controversies have arisen from the presence of Unitarians on the annual Whitsuntide Walks. Although dissent was voiced as long ago as the 1970s, it is in recent years that the controversy has come to a head. In 1998, the declared intention of the local Unitarian Church to participate in the Stalybridge Walk led to fierce condemnation from one local Church of England priest, who withdrew the co-operation of his own congregation and also gave a public lecture on the heresy of Unitarianism. Holy Trinity Church, Stalybridge has also refused to participate in subsequent years. Similarly, in 2004, when it was the turn of the Unitarian congregation in Dukinfield to lead the local Walk and thus gain the right to preach during a united service on the Town Hall steps, two local Congregationalist churches withdrew their participation. It was made clear that they would not take part in a 'Walk of Christian Witness' led by a 'non-Christian congregation' (*Tameside Reporter*, 3 June 2004: 2).

The Non-Subscribing Presbyterian Church of Ireland

Another means of determining the extent to which British Unitarianism can be considered as part of the Christian religion is to assess its relationship with a body that has an affiliated status within the General Assembly itself. The Non-Subscribing Presbyterian Church of Ireland (NSPCI) has, since the foundation of the General Assembly in 1928, been associated with the Assembly, its congregations having the individual right to attend and vote at GA meetings. The NSPCI traditionally educated its ministers at the mainland British colleges where Unitarians were trained, and the Moderator of the NSPCI was traditionally allocated a seat on the Council of the General Assembly. During much of the twentieth century, a number of the congregations of the NSPCI labelled themselves individually as 'Unitarian'.

In recent years, especially since the acknowledgement by British Unitarianism of its theological diversity, encapsulated in the change of the Objects of the General Assembly in 2001, there has been a greater distance between the two bodies. The NSPCI is unarguably a Christian Church, as asserted unambiguously in its *Code of Discipline*, a document drawn up in 1910 and still in current usage. Article One of the Constitution states

> *That the Scriptures of the Old and New Testament are the Rule of Christian Faith and Duty under the teaching of our Lord Jesus Christ.*
> (NSPCI, 1949: 7)

The only two congregations of the NSPCI that now continue to use the label 'Unitarian' are those in the Irish Republic. It is now some years since ministers of the NSPCI were trained in Unitarian establishments in England. The common ministerial Roll, whereby NSPCI ministers were accredited also by the Unitarian General Assembly, is no longer in use, and a number of NSPCI ministers are recognised, at their request, only by the NSPCI itself. These include a recent Moderator, Rev. Norman Hutton. The vacant ministries in the Irish churches, once included in a list of all vacancies in the United Kingdom and Ireland and circulated to all ministers on the Roll of the General Assembly, are no longer included. Discussions have been taking place for several years between Officers of the General Assembly and the NSPCI to establish a new form of working relationship, recognising the complete independence of one from the other. Thus, in the eyes of the NSPCI at least, British Unitarianism is no longer an integral part of the Christian religion.

If there is some discomfort within mainstream Christianity about the theological status of British Unitarianism, and if there is disagreement within Unitarianism itself, then the conclusion must be drawn that British Unitarianism can no longer consider itself as part of the Christian religion. If it is not, then some consideration must be given to the question of what status it does have, and whether or not it can be considered a religion in its own right.

Unitarianism as a religion

Definitions of religion

How one defines a religion will inevitably determine how far Unitarianism can consider itself as a religion alongside other religions. The *Shorter Oxford English Dictionary* defines a religion simply as 'a particular system of faith and worship' (Onions, 1968: 1697). This would enable almost any religious organisation to describe itself as a religion. To find a deeper definition, it is necessary to consider the work of scholars such as Emile Durkheim (1858–1917). Durkheim defined a religion as a system of beliefs and practices 'which connects all those attending in one moral community' (1912: 65). This definition emphasises the social aspects of religion: a religion is a particular collective process by a group of people. Hans le Grand, a Unitarian minister serving in the Netherlands, made the case that, according to Durkheim's definition, British Unitarianism, together with its sister movement in the United States, is a distinct religion.

> *They are groups of people, who together focus on spirituality, having worship services in churches, praying and meditating together, discussing religious issues and formulating moral stances. It is also clear that in this definition, Unitarianism is one religion.* (le Grand, 2002: 40)

Another way of defining religion is to see it as a system that seeks to wrestle with the ultimate problems of life and death.

> *It expresses their refusal to capitulate in the face of death, to give up in the face of frustration, to allow hostility to tear apart human associations.* (Yinger, 1970:7)

Using this definition also allows Unitarianism to consider itself as a religion in its own right. Unitarianism is very strongly focused on struggling with the ultimate problems of life and death. The website of the General Assembly suggests that matters of ultimate concern are of great importance to Unitarians. 'Everyone has the right to seek truth and meaning for themselves' (General Assembly, 2004b). Admittedly, Unitarians express their ultimate concerns in different ways, and even admit to different ultimate concerns. Nevertheless, if wrestling with the ultimate issues of life defines a religion, then, under those terms, Unitarianism can be classified as a religion. Le Grand admitted that the lack of a core set of beliefs is a problem for some in defining Unitarianism as a religion. He argued, however, that its lack of a core set of beliefs was what made Unitarianism distinctive, and that it therefore was more able to stand alone as a religion with an identifiable and unique role to play (le Grand, 2002:46).

It is also in practical terms that Unitarianism can identify itself as a religion. Paul Weller has made a contribution to the issue of self-identity that is also relevant to this issue. How a movement expresses itself through practice based on belief, he said, is what determines its distinctive religious nature.

> *Religion is perhaps best understood as a way of living in which some form of 'identification' (either in a weaker and more general sense, or in a stronger and specific sense of alignment with particular movements, communities and/or organisational forms) is often (though not always or necessarily) to be found in conjunction with different forms of 'believing' (in various combinations of certain values, ideals and/or doctrines) and can be*

expressed through 'practice' (that is related to shared symbols, rituals, observances and ethical orientations). (Weller, 2003: 57-81)

Objections to the classification of Unitarianism as a religion

Seeking to define Unitarianism simply according to a scholarly critique is insufficient. It is necessary to consider how others would consider Unitarianism in the light of the claims made for it, and to assess how Unitarianism compares with other systems of belief and practice that are recognised as religions.

One possible objection to the classification of Unitarianism as a religion is that it has no communal beliefs of its own but has simply adopted various beliefs from the more congenial traditions within several other religions. It thus has the best of all worlds. The statement in itself may be true, but it is the case that a number of religions have emerged from the development of a certain element of a different religion. Christianity, for example, shares the Hebrew scriptures with the Jewish religion and considers the role of Jesus as fulfilling the requirements of Jewish prophecy (see, for example, Luke 21: 22). The Bahá'í religion began life as a sect within Shia Islam, but developed into a distinctive system that drew on elements from various religions (Goring, 1994: 54). Sikhism grew out of a combination of elements from Hinduism and Islam (*ibid.*: 485). To say that Unitarianism could not qualify for the status of religion on the grounds that it contains a mixture of ideas and beliefs from other religions is to ignore the reality that other religions too are mixtures and amalgams of beliefs and practices from various cultures.

A second objection to the classification of Unitarianism as a religion is that there is too much diversity within it for it to be clearly enough identified. Again, this objection could be directed at other religions. For example, the 'suggestions of magic and mystery' within Tibetan Buddhism (Snelling, 1990: 92) are a vast contrast to the starkness and simplicity of the Theravada tradition of Buddhism. Hinduism, also, is so diverse as to allow within itself different doctrines that are mutually contradictory. The monism of the Advaita Vedanta school, for example, with its claims that Brahman is the only reality and that all else is illusion, is a total contrast to the philosophy of schools such as the Nyaya-Vaisheshika, with its exposition of the atomic theory and its detailed classification of reality (Werner, 1994: 168).

A third objection directed towards Unitarianism is that the movement is not united by beliefs at all, but by values. This again is not an unrepresentative statement of the Unitarian position. It does not mean that it is not a religion in its own right, however. A religion can be united in its values rather than its beliefs, as exemplified by the Jewish religion, a case of 'belonging without believing'. There is very little to unite the Jewish faith in terms of actual doctrine, but much to unite it in terms of tradition and culture. The Reconstructionist tradition, for instance, identifies the Jewish religion not so much by its historic teachings as by its existence as a dynamic religious civilisation, affirmed in the moral law agreed upon by all Jews. The details of the religion itself are to be discovered individually in the spirit of free enquiry (Brookes, 1974: 10).

Another objection to the classification of Unitarianism as a religion is that, as some individual Unitarians may claim to be Christians, or Buddhists, or Pagans, then they cannot claim Unitarianism as their religion without thus affirming adherence to more than one religion. If Christianity, for example, is a person's religion, the argument goes, then Unitarianism cannot also be their religion. If they made such a claim, they would be declaring themselves as followers of two distinctly different religious paths. This objection takes for granted, however, that it is reasonable to acknowledge allegiance to only one religion at any one time. As history has shown, it is possible to be an adherent of more than one religion at the same time, and there are some significant examples of this position. One major example can be found in Japan. For centuries it has been common for Japanese families to adhere to both Shinto and Buddhism. There are families today who belong to Buddhist organisations while at the same time paying homage to their family Shinto shrines at home. In China too, as already mentioned, there may be concurrent adherence to Buddhism, Confucianism, and Taoism. Similarly, there are Roman Catholics of Central and South America who are loyal to African-based religious traditions such as Voudoun and Santería.

The notion of adhering to more than one religion at a time is also acknowledged in the United Kingdom. One British Anglican priest, born into a Hindu family, has expressed his difficulties in freeing himself from his long cultural associations with the religion of his upbringing. He is thus able to identify with Hinduism on cultural terms, while at the same time identifying with Christianity on doctrinal terms (Sen, 2002: 120-21).

David Hart, an academic and Anglican priest, has asserted his belief that being part of both the Christian and Hindu communities has contributed to his understanding of himself, and he has expressed his gratitude for the opportunities offered to him by both fellowships of believers 'to join their family and become one of them' (Hart, 2002:126). Raimundo Pannikar is another example of someone seeking to bring together insights from both the Hindu and Roman Catholic traditions. As can be seen, then, the possibility of defining oneself as adhering to two religions at the same time is not without precedent.

It has thus been demonstrated that there are ways of answering the objections to the classification of Unitarianism as a religion in its own right. But what advantages are there in such a definition? That is what the next section of the study seeks to answer.

The advantages of religious status

To decide whether or not British Unitarianism can define the belief system to which it adheres as a religion in its own right is merely an academic exercise unless it can be shown that there are practical advantages to possessing such a status. These are the issues that British Unitarianism needs to deal with as it reflects on its relationships both with mainstream Christianity and with other world religions.

First, by defining itself as a distinct religion, Unitarianism is able to pursue dialogue further by being unfettered by unfavourable aspects of Christianity that obstruct closer ties with other faiths. Examples of such difficulties include the long history of prejudice directed at the Jewish religion, much of which was instigated by the Christian Church. The wearing of a badge to distinguish someone as a Jew and the creation of the Ghetto were both inventions, not of twentieth-century German Nazis, but of mediaeval Christian Church Councils (Domnitz, 1967: 82-3). Much has been done already by Unitarians to identify common ground with Judaism (Chryssides, 1998:77), but by virtue of being outside the Christian mainstream, they have greater freedom to develop these still further. Also, dialogue between Muslims and Christians is hampered by the fierce disagreements concerning the nature of the godhead. The Qur'an is unequivocal about the human status of Jesus and the unity of God (Sura 4: 171). In the opinion of both Muslims and traditional Christians, as far as theology is concerned, there can be no meeting ground so long as this disagreement cannot be resolved.

So in all seriousness we have to ask if this is not the end of the road as far as Christian–Muslim dialogue is concerned. And the answer must be, yes, as long as the conversation is conducted purely on the level of dogmatic, theological concepts. (Cracknell, 1984:48)

Unitarians have already taken steps, in major discussions held in 1992 and 1993, to make closer contacts with members of the Islamic faith (Marshall, 1999: 54). Freed from associations with mainstream Christianity, there would be greater opportunity to explore parallel theological concepts.

A second advantage of defining itself as a religion in its own right is that Unitarianism could then further its claim to be a spiritual home for three distinct constituencies. These include those who are alienated from any kind of traditional religious activity but would be attracted to a body not identifiable with any of the other religious bodies in the community: a religion for the 'non-religious'. This is the stance adopted by many Unitarian Universalists in the United States (Bartlett and Bartlett, 1990). It would also include those with a negative feeling about Christianity. It would further include those who do adhere to another religion but would, as mentioned earlier, feel able to follow two paths. This is a facility encouraged by Unitarian Universalists in the United States, where the distance from Christianity is much greater and where it is not unusual for members of, for example, the Hindu religion to be members also of a Unitarian Universalist congregation (Young, undated).

A third advantage of Unitarianism's definition as a religion is that it could create a distinct pastoral role for itself, free from the pressures of traditional religion. One of the services sometimes offered by Unitarian churches in Britain is the blessing of same-sex partnerships, which has been promoted more openly in recent years (Gould, 1996). There is even a written service produced for such occasions (Hill, 1993: 63-8). It is interesting to speculate, however, what greater impact the movement could have on that constituency if any associations with Christianity, with its perceived tradition of intolerance towards gay and lesbian people, were removed. Also, the conservative view on the indissolubility of marriage, expressed in most of the world's formal religions, has meant that many couples whose marriages have failed have felt unable to seek a religious dimension to the dismantling of their relationship. Again, the British Unitarian movement has the facility for meeting this need, with its service for the recognition of the end of a marriage (Hill, 1993: 91-6) (the service for which the author of the book received the award mentioned in an earlier chapter). One could speculate that by distancing itself further from traditional religious attitudes towards marriage, Unitarianism may have a significant service to offer. By defining itself as distinct, and thereby distant equally from all other religions, Unitarianism could have a greater claim to its role of offering adherents of the different religious traditions space to participate in pastoral situations where family pressures may otherwise come into play. These include, for example, rites of passage for families whose members come from different religious traditions; counselling that is free of dogmatic religious principles, yet offered with a religious dimension; and educational facilities removed from the negative moral or dogmatic associations with other religions.

Even without defining itself as a distinct religion, Unitarianism could claim many of these ideas. Defining Unitarianism as a distinct religion, however, affords the opportunity to be more creative, to start again to find within the community the opportunities for religious adventure unburdened by associations with the past, where people of mixed background can make use of pastoral facilities on an equal footing. There would be a price to pay. There would need to be a different type of relationship with Christian congregations, with the Christian ecumenical movement, and with the 'sister' denomination, the Non-Subscribing Presbyterian Church of Ireland. The Christian Unitarian tradition would need to be acknowledged as part of the historical background of the movement, rather than as a basis from which ideas are drawn and updated and interpreted.

Conclusion:
a new kind of Unitarianism?

The British Unitarian movement has had a long history of seeking to understand the major religions of the world, to learn from them, and to engage constructively with them. Whether intentionally or not, there is no doubt that those relationships have affected the way in which Unitarianism is practised. There is every reason to believe that British Unitarianism will continue to deepen its associations with other religions, and the insights gained from such encounters must surely continue to affect Unitarian faith and practice. Those changes could be fundamental and pose a tremendous challenge to Unitarians' perceptions of themselves. It remains to be seen whether British Unitarians are prepared for the adventure, and how they will respond to the challenges and opportunities laid before them. What will develop is a new kind of Unitarianism, a form of religion that is in constant flux, veering one way and another as it seeks to respond to ever-changing pressures and trends. If the British Unitarian movement can formulate out of its uncertainties a definition of itself that expresses a healthy relationship both with mainstream Christianity and with other world religions, then an uncertain future will be transformed into a confident one.

I conclude this study with a quotation from a popular hymn written by the late John Storey (1935-1997) which seeks to create the attitude so necessary to redefining British Unitarianism for the age in which we live:

Now new times demand new measures,
  And new ways we must explore;
Let each faith bring its own treasures
  To enrich the common store.
Then no more will creeds divide us –
  Though we love our own the best –
For the larger view will guide us
  As we join in common quest.
(Knight, 1985:126)

Appendix 1:
Results of the questionnaire

120 questionnaires were sent to Unitarian ministers and accredited lay leaders, and 80 were returned.
The results are as follows.

1. **To which inter-faith organisation(s) do you belong?**

    International Association for Religious Freedom 30

    World Congress of Faiths 10

    Council of Christians and Jews 16

    Interfaith Network. 1

    Other (local groups) 18

2. **Do you hold (or have you held) office in any inter-faith organisation at national or local level?**

    Yes 32   No 31

    If so, which?

    (a) At local level:

    Chair/President 7

    Secretary 7

    Treasurer 1

    Committee 16

    (b) At national level:

    Chair/President 4

    Secretary 1

    Treasurer 0

    Committee 7

3. **In what other practical ways do you pursue inter-faith dialogue?**
All-faith services 37
Inter-faith social events. 45
Attendance at other places of worship 45
Joint campaigns on social/political issues 26
Other: attending conferences 2, inter-faith retreats 1,
meditation groups 2, lectures 1

4. **With which religion, if any, do you dialogue the most or most effectively?**
Judaism. 35
Islam 11
Hinduism 22
Buddhism 25
Sikhism 11
Paganism 14
Other: Bahá'í 6, Shinto 2, Taoism 1, Brahma Kumaris 1, Rastafarians 1

5. **Which religion(s), apart from Christianity, have you studied seriously?**
Judaism. 48
Islam 27
Hinduism 36
Buddhism 46
Sikhism 11
Paganism 11
Other: Zen 2, Shinto 2, Rastafarianism 2, Zoroastrianism 1, Taoism 1,
Chinese Religion 1, Mormonism 1, Bahá'í 1, African Religion 1

6. **At which level have you studied World Religions?**
Personal study. 52
GCSE. 1
'A' level. 1
Degree. 25
Postgraduate Study. 18
Other: Ministerial training 16, Denominational lay training 3

7. **Do you practise any devotional techniques drawn from any non-Christian religion(s)? If so, which techniques?**

   Meditation. 44

   Reading of sacred texts 41

   Rituals 13

   Other: Wedding rites 1

8. **Do you feel that your personal faith has been influenced in any way by knowledge of the teachings or practices of other religions?**

   Yes 67   No 5

9. **In what ways, if any, do you mark the calendars of other religions?**

   Reference made in Sunday services 58

   Reference made in congregational newsletter/magazine 24

   Use of specific prayers/readings in worship. 51

   Special ritual, privately or in public worship 18

   Personal reflection or meditation 28

   No reference is made to the calendars of other religions. 7

   Other: Sunday School 1

10. **Do you bring the teachings of other world religions into your preaching?**

    Yes 71   No 4

11. **Do you use the sacred writings of other religions, or the works of modern religious teachers, in your services?**

    Yes 71   No 7

12. **Are there any other, particularly practical, ways in which your knowledge of other world religions has influenced your pastoral practice?**

    Inter-faith weddings 5, inter-faith funerals 2, practices for use with sickness & death 3, Jewish death anniversary 1, other rites of passage 4, counselling 4, exhibitions 1, hospitality for interfaith events 1, pastoral weekends 1, other faiths' material for stories 2, chaplaincy 2, face-to-face encounters 2.

13. Is British Unitarianism still primarily a liberal Christian denomination?
Yes 42   No 23   Don't know 10

If not, how would you define it?
Universalist 21
Pan-Religionist 1
Pluralist 12
Inclusivist 19
Humanitarian 14
Other: Humanist 1, Post-Christian 1

14. Do you feel that inter-faith dialogue has had an impact upon Unitarian faith and practice?
Yes 63   No 8

15. Is there a particular individual, group, or organisation that has been influential in changing the theological position of British Unitarianism?
James Martineau & Joseph Estlin Carpenter 5
Richard Boeke 2
Will Hayes 2
Arthur Long 1
Frank Clabburn 1
German theologians 1
Unitarian feminists 1
Transcendentalism 4
Panentheism 1
Buddhist spirituality 1
New Age spirituality 1
Unitarian Universalism 6
IARF* 4
Unitarian Renewal Group 4
Unitarian Christian Association 2
The Inquirer. 2

World Congress of Faiths 1
Development Skills Course 1
Unitarian Earth Spirit Network 2
Essex Hall 1
Sea of Faith 1
Humanism 1
(*International Association for Religious Freedom)

16. **Where would you place yourself on the Unitarian theological spectrum?**
Liberal Christian 28
Non-Christian Theist 10
Religious Humanist 6
Universalist/Pan-Religionist 12
Pragmatist 0
New Age Unitarian 0
Neo-Pagan 2
Other:
    Non-Realist 1
    Spiritual Humanist 1
    Pluralist 1
    Religious Humanist/Universalist 2
    Liberal Christian/Religious Humanist 1
    Liberal Christian/Non-Christian Theist 1
    Liberal Christian/Universalist 1
    Liberal Christian/Humanist/Universalist 1
    Liberal Christian/Non-Christian Theist/Humanist 1
    Liberal Christian/Universalist/Neo-Platonic 1
    Liberal Christian/Non-Christian Theist/Humanist/Universalist . . 1
    Non-Christian Theist/Pragmatist 1
    Non-Christian Theist/Universalist 1
    Non-Christian Theist/Universalist/Neo-Pagan 1
    Non-Christian Theist/Universalist/Humanist 1
    Non-Christian Theist/Humanist/Universalist/Pragmatist/
    Free Spiritualist 1

Panentheist/Creation Spirituality 1
Neo-Pagan/Universalist. 1
Humanist/New Age 1
Liberal Christian/Universalist/New Age/Neo-Pagan. 1

Please tick the appropriate boxes below:

(a) Sex:
Male 58
Female. 22

(b) Status:
Minister 67
Lay Pastor 7
Lay Leader 3
Student 3

(c) Work position:
In service 42
Retired. 26
Part-time. . . . . 7 (plus 5 without appointment)

(d) Age group:
25–40. 4
41–50. 10
51–65. 36
65 and above. 30

(e) Geographical position:
Scotland 3
North England 43
South England 17
Central England 10
Wales. 4
Overseas 3

Respondents

Rev. J. D. Allerton, BA, BD, MTh – Minister, Bury & Ainsworth
Rev. E. W. S. Baker, BA (Theol.) – Retired Minister
M. Barratt – Retired Lay Leader, now deceased
Rev. J. Barton, BA – Minister, Brighton & Worthing
Rev. B. J. Batchelor, BA – Retired Minister
Rev. G. W. Bennett, ALAM – Retired Minister
Rev. A. H. Birtles, BA – Retired Minister
Rev. J. Boeke, MDiv – Retired Minister
Rev. R. Boeke, BSc, MDiv, MA, DMin – Minister, Horsham
R. Booth, LLB, PhD – Lay Pastor, Bridport
Rev. R. A. Boyes, BA – Retired Minister
Rev. A. Bradley, BA, MA – Minister, Knutsford & Styal
Rev. E. W. Breeze, MA – Minister, Hyde Chapel & Flowery Field
Rev. B. Catherall, BA – Minister, Bolton Bank Street
Rev. B. S. Cockroft – Minister, Non-Subscribing Presbyterian Church of Ireland
Rev. J. Croft, BA, MA, MTh – Retired Minister
V. Curren – Retired Lay Pastor
Rev. M. Dadson, BA – Minister, Macclesfield & Newcastle (Staffs)
Rev. J. W. Darlison, BA, MA – Minister, Dublin
Rev. S. W. Dick – General Assembly Chief Executive
E. Dixon – Retired Lay Pastor
Rev. D. Doel, MA, PhD – Retired Minister
Rev. A. C. Fitzpatrick – Retired Minister
A. Fletcher, BSc, MA – Retired Lay Pastor
Rev. C. Goacher, BA – Minister, Derby & Belper
Rev. P. B. Godfrey, BA, DD – Retired Minister
Rev. J. L. Gould, AB, MA – Minister, Dean Row and Hale Barns
Rev. J. N. Harley, BA – General Assembly Youth Officer
Rev. A. Hills - Retired Minister
Rev. K. Hill – Retired Minister
Rev. P. L. Hughes, BSc – Minister, Atherton
Rev. W. T. Hughes, BA – Retired Minister (since deceased)
M. A. Jarrett – Former Lay Leader, Taunton
Rev. P. F. Johnson – Retired Minister
Rev. G. Jones – Retired Minister
Rev. J. E. Jones, BA – Retired Minister
Rev. M. A. Joyce, BA – Retired Minister
Rev. M. Kirk, BA, MA – Minister, York & Whitby
Rev. A. Latham – Retired Minister
Rev. L. Latham, MA – Retired Minister
Rev. C. Llwyd – Minister in secular employment

Rev. H. J. McLachlan, BA, MA, BD, DPhil – Retired Minister (since deceased)
Rev. A. F. McNeile, BA – Retired Minister
Rev. J. McNeile – Minister, Padiham
Rev. V. Marshall, MA, MPhil, BTh, BD, DMin – Minister, Dukinfield & Denton
Rev. C. Midgley, BA, BA – Minister, Altrincham & Urmston
Rev. J. A. Midgley, MA, MEd, BD, Minister, Manchester Cross Street
Rev. H. Mills – Minister, Hindley
Rev. D. K. Monk, BSc, MA – Minister, Hindley
J. Morgan – Lay Leader, Wick, Wales
Rev. G. J. Murphy, BA, MA – Retired Minister
Rev. F. MacC. O'Connor, BA – Minister, London Golders Green
Rev. A. R. Parker, BTh – Stalybridge & Failsworth
Rev. A. M. Parker – Retired Minister
Rev. A. Peart, MA, PhD – Principal, Unitarian College, Manchester
Rev. J. Pettitt, MA – Minister, Sheffield Fulwood
Rev. C. M. Reed, BA – Minister, Ipswich, Bedfield & Framlingham
Rev. D. J. Reynolds, BSc – Minister in secular employment
Rev. K. B. Ridgway – Retired Minister
Rev. P. J. Roberts, MA – Retired Minister
Rev. F. Schulman, BA, STB, DMin, DPhil, BD, MLitt – Retired Minister
    (since deceased)
Rev. P. Shaw – Minister, Mossley
C. C. Sinclair – Lay Pastor, Doncaster
Rev. D. F. Skelton – Retired Minister
B. Smith – Retired Lay Pastor
Rev. D. Smith – Retired Minister
Rev. L. Smith, MA, PhD, DD – Retired Minister
Rev. A. Stewart, BA, PhD – Minister, Leicester
Rev. D. Stirman – Retired Minister
Rev. R. Tarbuck – Retired Minister
Rev. C. P. P. Travis, MA – Minister, Leeds
C. M. Turnage – Retired Lay Pastor
Rev. D. A. Usher, MA. DMin – Minister, Sevenoaks & Godalming
Rev. G. R. Usher, BA, MA – Minister, Sheffield Upper Chapel
Rev. F. C. M. VanDenBroeder, BSc – Minister, Monton
Rev. R. Walder, BSc, MSc, PhD – Minister seeking settlement
Rev. F. Walker, BA – Retired Minister
Rev. C. M. Wicker, BA, PhD – Retired Minister
Rev. C. Wilson – Associate Minister, Great Yarmouth & Norwich
Rev. P. Womersley, MA – Retired Minister

Appendix 2:
Two 'inter-faith' hymns
by Andrew Hill

(referred to in Chapter 4)

Let us welcome

1. Let us welcome Channukah,
    Jewish feast of light,
   When quite unexpected
    And midst desperate plight,
   Came to tired people
    With their spirits low
   Plentiful resources
    Of God's love to show.
   Alleluia! Alleluia!
   Peace on earth, goodwill everyone.
   Alleluia!

2. Let us welcome Yuletide
    In this northern clime
   When in deep December
    Once again it's time
   For us to make merry
    And the long nights spurn;
   Bid the short days lengthen
    And the sun return.
   (Chorus)

3. Let us welcome Christmas
    when an infant smiles
   and from manger cradle
    gently reconciles
   all whose hearts are broken,
   or who live with pain,
    so that every person
    may be whole again.
   (Chorus)

4. At this festive season
    let us all rejoice,
   send the world a message
    with a common voice.
   Let our festive greeting
    be that wars shall cease
   and that all earth's people
    learn to live in peace.
    (Chorus)

Carol of the East

Shudd-ho-dana the King and Queen Maya his wife,
They set out on a journey, the journey of life;
And they came to a grove, where the virgin queen bore
Gotama the Buddha, whose heart's evermore.
I am part of the whole, of the whole I'm a part
So with friends and with neighbours I'll lift up my heart.

Great Tall King and his wife had eight girls, but no son
So that when one was born, something new was begun.
Kung-fu-tze, the great heart, he was born on that night,
'Analects' he would make, and the people do right.
I am part of the whole, of the whole I'm a part
So with friends and with neighbours I'll lift up my heart.

Now when Joseph and Mary to Bethlehem came
And sweet Jesus, their dear heart, was born to great fame,
Three kings and four shepherds came by specially
And dear Mary she pondered her heart motherly.
I am part of the whole, of the whole I'm a part
So with friends and with neighbours I'll lift up my heart.

Bibliography

Adler, M. (1979) *Drawing Down the Moon*, Boston, USA: Beacon Press

Adler, M. (1996) 'Vibrant, Juicy, Contemporary: or, Why I am a UU Pagan', http://moonpathcuups.org/margot.htm

d'Alviella, Count E. Goblet (1886) *The Contemporary Evolution of Religious Thought in England, America and India*, London: Williams & Norgate

Alger, W. R. (1857) 'Extracts from Poetry of the East', *The Living Age*, Volume 52, Issue 668 (14 March)

Alger, W. R. (1860, reissued 1968) *A Critical History of a Doctrine of a Future Life*, New York: Greenwood

Armstrong, R. A. (1870) 'Buddhism and Christianity', *The Theological Review*, no. 7, pp.176–200

Armstrong, R. A. (1881) 'Hopes and dangers of English Unitarianism', *The Inquirer*, 30 June, pp.3–4

Arnold, Sir E. (1908) *The Light of Asia*, London: Kegan, Paul, Trench, Trübner

Barr, M. (1937) *The Great Unity*, London: Lindsey Press

Barraclough, J. (2003) 'Students for the Ministry', *Counterpoint* (General Assembly of Unitarian and Free Christian Churches), p.3

Barraclough, J. (2004) 'A Buddhist meditational practice', *The Journal of the Unitarian Ministry*, pp.13–14

Bartlett, J. R. and L.E. Bartlett (1990) 'A Religion for the "Non-Religious"',Berkeley, California: private publication

Baxter, L. *et al.* (eds.) (1991) *Hymns of Faith and Freedom*, London: Chalice Press

BBC (2004) 'Religion and Ethics – Quakers', www.bbc.co.uk/religion/religions/christianity/subdi/introduction.shtm

Bell, J. (1970) 'Encounter with change', *IARF: the Twentieth Congress*, 67/68, Spring, p.29, IARF Information Service

Belsham, T. (1811) *A Calm Inquiry into the Scripture Doctrine Concerning the Person of Christ*, London: Lindsey Press

Benton, A. (1978) 'A kind of ministry: contact with the Sikh community', *The Journal of the Unitarian Ministry*, pp.10–13

Besant, A. (1894) 'Theosophy', *The Daily Chronicle* (April 9)

Blavatsky, H. P. (undated) *Studies in Occultism*, Point Loma, California: Theosophical University Press

Boeke, R. (1996) 'An American on the Sea of Faith', *The Journal of the Unitarian Ministry* (unpaginated)

Boeke, R. (2002) 'Ugly duckling or swan? Is Unitarianism a universal religion?' in M. Smith (ed.) *Prospects for the Unitarian Movement*, pp.19–28, London: Lindsey Press

Boeke, R. (2003) *Many Paths, One Reality*, Berkeley, California: Unitarian Universalist Church

Bolam, C. G., J. Goring, *et al.* (1968) *The English Presbyterians*, London: George Allen and Unwin

Booth, J. N. (1986) *Introducing Unitarian Universalism*, Boston, MA: Unitarian Universalist Association

Bowden, J. (1990) *Who's Who in Theology*, London: SCM Press

Bradley, A. (1995) *Why I Am Still a Unitarian*, London: Newington Green Unitarian Church

Braybrooke, M. (1992) *Pilgrimage of Hope*, New York: Crossroad

British and Foreign Unitarian Association (1851) *Annual Report*, London: BFUA

British and Foreign Unitarian Association (1883) *Unitarian Almanack*, London: BFUA

British and Foreign Unitarian Association (1902) *The Essex Hall Hymnal*, London: Philip Green

British and Foreign Unitarian Association (1905) *The New Hymnal*, London: Novello

Brookes, R. S. (1974) *Sects in Judaism*, Birmingham: The Singers Hill Hebrew Congregation

de Brosses, C. (reprinted 1972) *Du Cultes des Dieux Fétiches*, Farnborough: Gregg International Press

Brotherhood of the Cross and Star (2003) 'The BCS: A Brief Introduction', http://freespace.virgin.net/dolly.daniels/ARTICLES/briefintr.htm

Buckle, D. (ed.) (1999) *Sources of Worship Material*, London: General Assembly of Unitarian and Free Christian Churches

Burwasser, D. (1996) 'A Brief History of the Covenant of Unitarian Universalist Pagans', www.cuups.org/content/aboutcuups/history.html

Cambridge Unitarian Church (undated) *Who Are The Unitarians?*, Cambridge: Cambridge Unitarian Church

Carpenter, J. E. (1873) 'Letters of Joseph Estlin Carpenter in Palestine', London: private publication

Carpenter, J. E. (1882) 'The education of the ministry' in *Report of the National Conference of Unitarian, Free Christian Churches etc*, pp91–2, London: Williams & Norgate

Carpenter, J. E. (1893) 'The need of a wider conception of revelation' in J. H. Barrows (ed.) *The World's Parliament of Religions*, pp842–9, Chicago: Parliament

Carpenter, J. E. (1900) 'A Century of Comparative Religion, 1800–1900' (reprinted from *The Inquirer*), Oxford: private publication

Carpenter, J. E. (1906) 'How Japanese Buddhism appeals to a Christian Theist', *The Hibbert Journal* No 4, pp503–26

Carpenter, J. E. (1909) 'Things new and old' in W. C. Bowie (ed.) (1910) *Things New and Old*, pp1–24, London: British and Foreign Unitarian Association

Carpenter, J. E. (1910) 'Preface' in *The International Congress of Free Christianity and Religious Progress*, London: Inquirer Publishing Co.

Carpenter, J. E. (1911) *The Place of Christianity Among the Religions of the World*, London: Philip Green

Carpenter, J. E. (1912) *The Opportunity of the East*, supplement to *The Christian Commonwealth* (February)

Carpenter, J. E. (1913) *Comparative Religion*, London: Oxford University Press

Carpenter, J. E. (1921) *Theism in Medieval India: The Hibbert Lectures 1919*, London: Williams & Norgate

Carpenter, J. E. (1925) 'Introduction' in J. E. Carpenter (ed.) *Freedom and Truth*, pp3–19, London: Lindsey Press

Carpenter, L. (1833) *On Rajah Rammohun Roy*, London: Rowland Hunter and Marshall & Simpkin

Carpenter, M. (1875) *The Last Days in England of the Rajah Rammohun Roy*, London: E. T. Whitfield

Carpenter, R. L. (1848) *The Life of the Rev. Lant Carpenter*, London: Christian Tract Society

Carpenter, W. B. (1877) 'Sketch of the Life and Work of Mary Carpenter of Bristol', Bristol: private publication

Carter, G. (1902) *Unitarian Biographical Dictionary*, London: Unitarian Christian Publishing Office

Chalmers, A. (ed.) (1904) *Litanies and Chants*, Wakefield: Westgate Chapel

Channing, W. E. (1819) 'Unitarian Christianity' in W. E. Channing (1884) *The Complete Works of William Ellery Channing*, pp278–88, London and New York: Routledge

Charlesworth, S. (1903) *Memorials of Robert Spears 1825–1899*, Belfast: Ulster Unitarian Christian Association

Chryssides, G. D. (1988) *The Path of Buddhism*, Edinburgh: St. Andrew Press

Chryssides, G. D. (1998) *The Elements of Unitarianism*, Shaftesbury: Element

Chryssides, G. D. (1999) 'Unitarians, new religions, and the New Age' in G. D. Chryssides (ed.) *Unitarian Perspectives on Contemporary Religious Thought*, pp91–109, London: Lindsey Press

Chryssides, G. D. (2002) 'Unitarians and new religious movements' in M. F. Smith (ed.) *Prospects for the Unitarian Movement*, pp29–38, London: Lindsey Press

Clare, L. (1932) *Prayer: Its Method and Justification*, London: Lindsey Press

Clark, A. (2003) 'Declaration of Religious Freedom and Responsibility', *Newsletter of the IARF* (December), pp2–3

Clarke, J. F. (1871–1883) *Ten Great Religions* Volumes I and II, Boston, USA: Houghton Mifflin

Cohen, L. and L. Manion (1994) *Research Methods in Education*, London: Routledge

Conway, M. D. (ed.) (1876) *The Sacred Anthology: a Book of Sacred Scriptures*, London: Trübner

Crabtree, H. (1932) *Some Religious Cults and Movements of Today*, London: Lindsey Press

Cracknell, K. (1984) *Christians and Muslims Talking Together*, London: British Council of Churches

Croft, J. (ed.) (1984) *Growing Together*, London: General Assembly of Unitarian and Free Christian Churches

Crompton Jones, R. (ed.) (1898) *A Book of Prayer in Thirty Orders of Worship*, London: Williams and Norgate

Cross, F. L. (ed.) (1957) *The Oxford Dictionary of the Christian Church*, London: Oxford University Press

Daggers, J. (2002) *The British Christian Women's Movement: A Rehabilitation of Eve*, Aldershot: Ashgate

Davis, V. D. (ed.) (1927) *Prayers in Public Worship and in College Chapel by J. Estlin Carpenter*, London: Lindsey Press

Deacon, J. A. (1977) 'Joseph Estlin Carpenter: An Intellectual Biography', unpublished MA thesis, University of Lancaster

Dean, P. (1875) 'The minister's religious principles' in F.W. Newman, *Sin Against God* (unpaginated appendix), London: Trubner

Dickinson, J. (1984) 'How I Became a Bahá'í', *National Unitarian Fellowship Newsletter* (September), pp.6–8

Doel, D. C. (1990) *The Perennial Psychology*, London: Lindsey Press

Doel, D. C. (1992) *Out of Clouds and Darkness*, London: Lindsey Press

Doel, D. C. (1997) *The Lost Child and the Christ Child*, Dukinfield, Greater Manchester: Chapel Hill Press

Domnitz, M. (1967) *Judaism and Inter-Group Relations*, London: Board of Deputies of British Jews

Drummond, J. and C. B. Upton (eds.) (1902) *The Life and Letters of James Martineau* Volume I, London: James Nisbet

Durkheim, E. (1912) *Les Formes Elementaires de la Vie Religieuse*, Paris: Alcan

Eliot, S. A. (1907) 'Opening address of the President' in C.W. Wendte (ed.) *Freedom and Fellowship in Religion*, Boston, USA: International Congress of Religious Liberals

Elliott, J. (1994) 'Atmosphere and worship' in F. Hytch (ed.) *NUF 50: The First Half-Century of the National Unitarian Fellowship* pp47–8, London: Lindsey Press

Emerson, R. W. (1899) 'Blight', *Early Poems of Ralph Waldo Emerson*, New York, Boston: Thomas Y. Crowell and Company available at www.online-literature.com/ads/topad.php

Faber, H. (1936) 'Our growing task', *International Association for Liberal Christianity and Religious Freedom Bulletin*, No 19

Farnell, L. R. (1929) 'Comparative religion: Pali and the religions of India' in C.H. Herford (ed.) *Joseph Estlin Carpenter: A Memorial Volume*, pp162–78, Oxford: Clarendon Press

Firoozmand, M. (1984) 'Letter from a B'ahá'i', *National Unitarian Fellowship Newsletter* (September), pp9–10

Flower, J. C. (1922) 'Jesus' in A. Hall (ed.) *Aspects of Modern Unitarianism*, London: Lindsey Press

Foerster, L. A. (ed.) (2003) *For Praying Out Loud: Interfaith Prayers for Public Occasions*, Boston: Skinner House

Frazer, J. (1922) *The Golden Bough*, New York: Macmillan

Freud, S. (1962) *Totem and Taboo*, New York: W. Norton

General Assembly of Unitarian and Free Christian Churches (1932a) *Orders of Worship*, London: Lindsey Press

General Assembly of Unitarian and Free Christian Churches (1932b) *A Book of Occasional Services*, London: Lindsey Press

General Assembly of Unitarian and Free Christian Churches (1995) *Guidelines II: Ministerial Training and Development*, London: General Assembly

General Assembly of Unitarian and Free Christian Churches (1999) *Annual Report*, London: General Assembly

General Assembly of Unitarian and Free Christian Churches (2000) *Annual Report*, London: General Assembly

General Assembly of Unitarian and Free Christian Churches (2001) *Annual Report*, London: General Assembly

General Assembly of Unitarian and Free Christian Churches (2002) *Annual Report*, London: General Assembly

General Assembly of Unitarian and Free Christian Churches (2003) *Directory*, London: General Assembly

General Assembly of Unitarian and Free Christian Churches (2004a) *Seventy Years of GA Resolutions*, London: General Assembly Social Responsibility Panel

General Assembly of Unitarian and Free Christian Churches (2004b) 'British Unitarianism', www.unitarian.org.uk/unitarian ways.htm

General Assembly of Unitarian and Free Christian Churches (undated) *John Page Hopps*, London: Unitarian Press

Gilley, K. (ed.) (2002) 'Building Our Identity', London: Unitarian Renewal Group

Goacher, C. (2004) 'Profile: Ullet Road Church, Liverpool', *The Unitarian*, No. 1204 (May), pp.43–4

Godfrey, P. B. (ed.) (1976) *Unitarian Orders of Worship*, Sheffield: Upper Chapel

Godfrey, P. B. (1999) 'British involvement in the IARF', *IARF World* No. 2, pp7&12

Golders Green Unitarians (2003) Newsletter of the Congregation (June)

Gollancz, V. (ed.) (1950) *A Year of Grace*, London: Victor Gollancz

Gordon, A. (1970) *Heads of English Unitarian History*, Bath: Cedric Chivers

Goring, J. and R. Goring (1984) *The Unitarians*, Exeter: Religious and Moral Education Press

Goring, J. (2003) 'Brotherhood of the Cross and Star: A Personal View', http://freespace.virgin.net/dolly.daniels/ ARTICLES/bcsview.htm

Goring, R. (ed.) (1994) *Dictionary of Beliefs and Religions*, Edinburgh: Larousse

Gould, J. L. (1996) *Where We Stand: Gay and Lesbian Issues and the Unitarian and Free Christian Churches*, London, Unitarian General Assembly Information Department

Gow, H. (1928) *The Unitarians*, London: Methuen

Griffith, R. (1994) Sixth contributor in M. Smith (ed.) 'Unitarian Views of Earth and Nature', London: Unitarian Information Department

Hall, A. (1962) *Beliefs of a Unitarian*, London: Lindsey Press

Harris Manchester College, Oxford (1995) 'Ministerial Training: College Curriculum for Unitarian Students', Oxford: Harris Manchester College

Hart, D. A. (2002) 'Bridging a divide – Passing over the Ganges' in D.A. Hart (ed.) (2002) *Multi-Faith Britain*, Alresford, Hants: O Books

Hayes, W. (1929) *Leaves from the Larger Bible*, Dublin and Chatham: Order of the Great Companions

Hayes, W. (1931a) *Indian Bibles*, London: Friends of India

Hayes, W. (1931b) *How the Buddha Became a Christian Saint*, Dublin and Chatham: Order of the Great Companions

Hayes, W. (1931c) *Sweet Calumus*, Dublin and Chatham: Order of the Great Companions

Hayes, W. (ed.) (1932) *Temple Chimes: Thirty Three Poems of St .Thayumanavar* (translated by Surendranath Voegeli-Arya, SPY), Dublin and Chatham: Order of the Great Companions

Hayes, W. (1938a) *Unitarians of the United World*, Chatham: Order of the Great Companions

Hayes, W. (1938b) *The Stamper of the Skies: A Bible for Animal Lovers*, London: Order of the Great Companions

Hayes, W. (1954) *Every Nation Kneeling*, Chatham: Order of the Great Companions

Hayes, W. (undated) *The Great Mother*, London: The Free Religious Movement

Herford, C. H. (ed.) (1929) *Joseph Estlin Carpenter: A Memorial Volume*, Oxford: Clarendon Press

Hewett, P. (1955) An Unfettered Faith: The Religion of a Unitarian, London: Lindsey Press

Hewett, P. (1968) *On Being a Unitarian*, London: Lindsey Press

Hewett, P. (1992) *Understanding Unitarians*, London: Hibbert Trust

Higgins, R. (2003) 'Emerson at 200: Emerson's mirror' www.uuworld.org/2003/02/feature1a.html

High Pavement Chapel, Nottingham (1914) *The Order for the Communion Service*, Nottingham: High Pavement Chapel

Hill, A. M. (1993) (ed.) *Celebrating Life*, London: Lindsey Press

Hill, A. M. (1994) *The Unitarian Path*, London: Lindsey Press

Hill, A. M. (1995) 'William Adam: Unitarian missionary', *Transactions of the Unitarian Historical Society*, 21:1, pp30–42

Hill, A. M. (2004) 'Prayer for an interfaith service', *Journal of the Unitarian Ministry*, p15

Hirsch, E. (1893) 'The elements of universal religion' in J. H. Barrows (ed.) *The World's Parliament of Religions* II, pp1304–8 Chicago: Parliament

Hocking, W. E. (1940) *Living Religions and a World Faith*, New York: Macmillan

Holt, R. V. (1938) *The Unitarian Contribution to Social Progress in England*, London: George Allen & Unwin

Holt, R. V. (ed.) (1945) *A Free Religious Faith: The Report of a Unitarian Commission*, London: Lindsey Press

Hosegood, L. M. (1972) *The Conduct of Worship: A Guide for Lay Preachers*, London: Lindsey Press

Hostler, J. (1981) *Unitarianism*, London: Hibbert Trust

Howlett, D. (1985) *The Unitarian Movement: Projections and Realities*, London: Unitarian Information

Hughes, C. and S. Storey (eds.) (2000) *The Common Quest: Selected Writings of John Andrew Storey*, London: Lindsey Press

Hughes, P. L. (ed.) (1987) *With Hands Together*, Macclesfield & Knutsford: Unitarian Ministerial Fellowship

Hume, D. (1757, reprinted 1957) (edited by H. E. Root) *The Natural History of Religion*, Stanford, California: Stanford University Press

Inter Faith Network for the UK (2003) 'Understanding With Integrity', www.ifnet-adsel.demon.co.uk/home.htm

Inter Faith Network for the UK (undated) Information Leaflet. London: IFNUK

International Association for Liberal Christianity and Religious Freedom (1958) *Congress Handbook*, Chicago: IALCRF

International Association for Religious Freedom (1969) 'Congress service', *IARF News Digest* No. 60, p34

International Association for Religious Freedom (1987) *Proceedings of the 1987 World Congress*, Frankfurt: IARF

Internet Encyclopedia of Philosophy (2003) 'Theosophy', *www.utm.edu/research/iep/t.theosoph.htm*

Inyang-Ebom, A. (2003) 'Beyond Prejudice', http://freespace.virgin.net/dolly.daniels/abinger/beyondpre.htm

Jones, T. H. (undated-a) *Suffer the Children*, London: Unitarian Religious Education Department

Jones, T. H. (undated-b) *Ignition*, London: Unitarian Religious Education Department

Jung, C. G. (1963) *Memories, Dreams, Reflections*, London: Flamingo

Kennedy, A. (1987) 'Hymns for Living', *Stirrings*, pp2–3, Unitarian College, Manchester

Kent, J. (1983) 'Unitarianism' in A. Richardson and J. Bowden (eds.) *A New Dictionary of Christian Theology*, London: SCM

Kenworthy, F. (ed.) (1964) *Unitarian Theology in 1964. Commission on Unitarian Faith and Action in the Modern World*, London: Unitarian General Assembly

Kenworthy, F. (ed.) (1966) *Unitarians Discuss Their Faith. Commission on Unitarian Faith and Action in the Modern World*, London: Unitarian General Assembly

Kielty, J. (1959) *British Unitarianism: Past, Present and Future*, Boston, Mass: Minns Lectureship Committee

Kirk, M. (2002) 'The future of Unitarian worship' in M.F. Smith (ed.) *Prospects for the Unitarian Movement*, London: Lindsey Press

Knight, S. H. (ed.) (1985) *Hymns for Living*, London: Lindsey Press

Lang, A. (1898) *Modern Mythology*, London: Longmans, Green

le Grand, J. B. (2002) 'Unitarianism: A proper religion?', *Faith and Freedom*, Volume 55, Pt 1, No. 154, pp38–47

Lester, A. (2000) 'Church is dead', *Journal of the Unitarian Ministry*, pp26–34

Ling, T. (1973) 'Max Weber in India', *The University of Leeds Review* (May), pp42–65

Lister, B. *et al.* (eds.) (undated) *Intermediate Department Teachers' Handbook*, London: Lindsey Press

Long, A. J. (1963) *Faith and Understanding*, London: Lindsey Press

Long, A. J. (1978) *Fifty Years of Theology 1928–1978: The Vindication of Liberalism*, London: Lindsey Press

Long, A. J. (1982) *Look Unto the Rock From Whence Ye Were Hewn*, London: General Assembly of Unitarian and Free Christian Churches

Long, A. J. (1986) 'The life and work of J. Estlin Carpenter' in B. Smith (ed.) *Truth, Liberty, Religion*, pp265–89, Oxford: Manchester College

Lovis, R. (1994) Plymouth Unitarian Church Calendar

Lowenstein, T. (1996) *The Vision of the Buddha*, London: Macmillan

Lubbock, J. (1872) *Prehistoric Times*, New York: Appleton

Lyngdoh, C. (1987) 'One hundred years of Unitarianism in North Eastern India' in D. Marbaniang (ed.) *Centenary Celebration: Unitarian Union North East India 1887–1987*, pp3–13, Megalaya: The Unitarian Union of North East India

McGuffie, D. (1982) *The Hymn Sandwich*, London: Unitarian Worship Sub-Committee

McLachlan, H. (1915) *The Unitarian Home Missionary College*, London: Sherratt & Hughes

McLachlan, H. (ed.) (1926) *College Services: For Use By The Unitarian College*, Manchester: Unitarian College

McNeile, A. (1993) 'Whither Unitarianism', *Stirrings*, pp.6–7, Unitarian College, Manchester

Malinowski, B. (1948) *Magic, Science and Religion*, Garden City, New York: Doubleday

Manchester College (1915) *Manchester College, Oxford: To Truth, to Liberty, to Religion*, Oxford: Manchester College

Marshall D. V. (1986) *Communion Service for Use in Unitarian Services*, Birmingham: Unitarian New Meeting

Marshall, D. V. (1990) 'Building on the past', *National Unitarian Fellowship Viewpoint* October, 94, pp1–7

Marshall, D. V. (1992) 'Tout est changement', *Journal of the Unitarian Ministry*, pp29–30

Marshall, D. V. (1993) 'James Freeman Clarke and comparative religion', *Faith and Freedom* Vol. 46 Part 2, No. 137, pp106–11

Marshall, D. V. (1995) 'A new language for worship', *Stirrings*, pp15–17, Unitarian College, Manchester

Marshall, D. V. (1996) 'Collects to the God of Many Names' in D. Monk (ed.) *Stirring Words for Reflection*, pp4–7, Manchester: Unitarian College

Marshall, D. V. (1998) 'Unitarian rites for the seasons', *New Age Unitarian Networkers' File* 2 (unpaginated)

Marshall, D. V. (1999) 'Unitarians and other religions' in G.D. Chryssides (ed.) *Unitarian Perspectives on Contemporary Religious Thought*, pp46–60, London: Lindsey Press

Marshall, D. V. (2001) 'The Work of Joseph Estlin Carpenter in the Field of Comparative Religion', MPhil thesis: Open University

Marshall, D. V. (2002) 'New forces shaping Unitarian thought' in M.F. Smith (ed.) *Prospects for the Unitarian Movement*, pp1–8, London, Lindsey Press

Marshall, D. V. (2003) 'World Religions', module for the Course in Lay Preaching and Conduct of Worship, London: General Assembly of Unitarian and Free Christian Churches

Marshall, D. V. (2004a) 'Your Marriage Ceremony', Dukinfield: private publication

Marshall, D. V. (2004b) 'A happy Sunfest to you all', *Unitarian Earth-Spirit Network File*, Issue no. 25 (Summer)

Marshall, D. V. (2004c) *In Praise of the Mystic Dancer*, Manchester: Provincial Assembly of Lancashire and Cheshire

Marshall, D. V. (2004d) 'A prayer based on words by Guru Arjan 1503–1606', *Journal of the Unitarian Ministry*, pp18–19

Martineau, J. (1853) 'The rationale of religious enquiry' in A. Hall (ed.) *James Martineau: Selections*, pp.61–62, London: Lindsey Press (1950)

Martineau, J. (ed.) (1879) *Ten Services of Public Prayer*, London: BFUA

Martineau, J. (1890) *The Seat of Authority in Religion*, London: Longmans, Green

Martineau, J. (1990) *A Study of Religion*, Oxford: Clarendon Press

Mascaro, J. (trans.) (1965) *The Upanishads*, London: Penguin

Mathur, A. P. (2003) 'Swami Ji Maharaj: His Life and Work', www.santmat-meditation.net/saints/bio-14.html

Medhurst, P. (1992) *Rammohun Roy and the Day-Star of Approaching Morn* (Essex Hall Lecture 1992), London: General Assembly of Unitarian and Free Christian Churches

Meher Baba Association (2003) 'Who is Meher Baba? His Life, his Work, his Call, his Spiritual Status', www.meherbaba.co.uk/whois.htm

Mellone, S. H. (1923) *Unitarian Teachers*, London: Lindsey Press

Mellone, S. H. (1925) *Liberty and Religion*, London: Lindsey Press

Meynell, K. (2003) 'What is Spiritualism?', www.snu.org.uk/spirit.htm

Midgley, J. A. (1975) 'Christianity and the encounter of world religions' in D.G. Wigmore-Beddoes (ed.) *Concerning Jesus*, pp.97–108, London: Lindsey Press

Midgley, J. A. (ed.) (1990) *Building Your Own Theology: The British Version*, London: Unitarian Renewal Group & the Unitarian General Assembly

Midgley, J. A. (ed.) (2000) *Reflections on the Ministry*, Manchester: Unitarian Ministerial Fellowship

Mill Hill Chapel, Leeds (1892) *Psalms, Canticles, and Anthems*, Leeds: Mill Hill Chapel

Mitchell, L. (ed.) (2000) *Unitarian Earth Spirit Network File*, Issue 8, Spring

Mitchell, L. (ed.) (2003) *Unitarian Earth Spirit Network File*, Issue 21, Summer

Monk, D. (1997) *Vipassana Meditation: The Path of Insight*, Bolton: Meditational Fellowship

Monk, D. (1999) *Emptiness*, Bolton: Meditational Fellowship

Monk, D. (2001) *Compassion*, Bolton: Meditational Fellowship

Monk, W. H. (ed.) (1916) *Hymns Ancient and Modern*, London: William Clowes

Moser, C. A. and G. Kalton (1971) *Survey Methods in Social Investigation*, London: Heinemann

Müller, F. M. (1856) *Comparative Mythology*, London: Longmans, Green

Murray, A. (ed.) 1999 *Sir William Jones 1746–94: A Commemoration*, Oxford: Oxford University Press

Nemoto, M. (1999) 'A Buddhist theological basis for inter-religious cooperation', *IARF World* No. 2, pp8–11

Nesbitt, E. (2003) *Interfaith Pilgrims: Living Truths and Truthful Living*, London: Quaker Books

New Chapel, Denton (2004) Bi-Monthly Calendar (July and August)

New Meeting House, Birmingham (1830) *Psalms and Hymns*, Birmingham: New Meeting House

Non-Subscribing Presbyterian Church of Ireland (1949) *The Constitution and Code of Discipline*, Belfast: NSPCI

Northern Federation for Training in Ministry (1997) *Course Handbook*, Manchester: Northern Federation

O'Connor, F. (2001) "What this Unitarian church is: a challenge to the Bishop of Oxford', *Stirrings* (Unitarian College, Manchester) pp10–12.

O'Connor, F. (2004) 'The World Congress of Faiths and Unitarianism', *Journal of the Unitarian Ministry*, pp25–7

Onions, C. T. (ed.) (1968) *The Shorter Oxford English Dictionary*, Oxford: Clarendon Press

Pagan Federation (2001) *The Pagan Federation Information Pack*, London: Pagan Federation

Parke, D. B. (ed.) (1985) *The Epic of Unitarianism*, Boston, USA: Skinner House

Parker, A. M. (2003) 'Those who do the work will know the doctrine', *Journal of the Unitarian Ministry*, pp25–7

Parker, T. (1864) 'The transient and permanent in Christianity', in W.C. Bowie, W. C. (ed.) (1908) *The Transient and Permanent in Religion*, pp1–36, London: British and Foreign Unitarian Association

Parker, T. (1876) *A Discourse of Matters Pertaining to Religion*, London: Trübner & Co.

Peacock, A. (1956) *Fellowship Through Religion*, London: World Congress of Faiths

Peart, A. (1999) 'Forgotten prophets: Unitarian women and religion' in G.D. Chryssides (ed.) *Unitarian Perspectives on Contemporary Religious Thought*, pp61–76, London, Lindsey Press

Primary Document (1892) 'The primary document of English Unitarianism 1682', *The Christian Life and Unitarian Herald*, October 29, p523

Pritchard, M. (ed.) (1905) *Monthly Notes for Sunday Classes*, London: Unitarian School Association

Ramanujan, A. K. (trans.) (1973) *Speaking of Siva*, Harmondsworth: Penguin

Ranck, S. (1986) *Cakes for the Queen of Heaven*, Boston, USA: Beacon Press

Redfern, L. and J.E. Wallace (eds.) (1930) *Psalms and Canticles of the Church*, Liverpool: Ullet Road Church

Religious Freedom Young Adult Network (2003) *IARF World* (January), p7

Rhadakrishnan, S. (trans.) (1950) *The Dhammapada*, Oxford: Oxford University Press

Richards, D. (1959) *Man's Adventure in the Discovery of God, Right and Freedom*, London: Unitarian General Assembly

Richardson, A. and J. Bowden (eds) (1983) *A New Dictionary of Christian Theology*, London: SCM

Roberts, P. (1989a) 'The challenge of psychism to contemporary Unitarianism', *The Journal of the Unitarian Society for Psychical Studies* No. 42, pp26–36

Roberts, P. (1989b) 'Roots of ministry', *Journal of the Unitarian Ministry*, pp27–30

Roberts, P. (2004) 'The limits of inter-faith', *Journal of the Unitarian Ministry*, pp5–7

Robertson, O. (2003) 'Fellowship of Isis Online Liturgy Booklet: Urania, Ceremonial Magic of the Goddess', www.fellowshipofisis.com/liturgy/urania5.html

Robinson, A. (1999) 'Keeping up with all the Joneses', *The Times Higher Education Supplement*, April 2, p21

Robinson, J. A. T. (1979) *Truth is Two-Eyed*, London: SCM Press

Ruston, A. (1999) 'Robert Spears – the nineteenth century Unitarian Dynamo', *Transactions of the Unitarian Historical Society*, Vol. XXII no.1 (April), pp54–67

Ruston, A. (2003) 'Robert Spears', www.uua.org/uuhs/duub/articles.robertspears.html

Ruston, A. (2004) 'Interfaithery', *Journal of the Unitarian Ministry*, pp.12–14

Sargant, N. C. (1987) 'Mary Carpenter in India', Bristol: private publication

Sastri, S. N. (1907) 'Theism in India' in W.C. Bowie (ed) *The Faith of a Free Church*, London: British and Foreign Unitarian Association

Sathya Sai Baba (2003) 'Works of Sai Baba', http://members.aol.com/introsai/works/index.htm

Seaburg, C. (ed.) (1993) *The Communion Book*, Boston, USA: Unitarian Universalist Ministers' Association

Seager, R. H. (1986) *The World's Parliament of Religions, Chicago, Illinois 1893: America's Coming of Age*, Cambridge, Mass: Harvard University

Seekers Way (2003) 'Radha Soami Satsang Beas: An Introduction' www.seekersway.org/seekersguide/radhasoami1g.html

Sen, A. (2002) 'Crossing boundaries – a Hindu–Christian biographical reflection' in D. A. Hart (ed.) *Multi-Faith Britain*, Alresford, Hants: O Books

Sen, A. K. (1967) *Raja Rammohun Roy: The Representative Man*, Calcutta: Sadharan Brahmo Samaj

Sharpe, E. J. (1975) *Comparative Religion: A History*, London: Duckworth

Shiels, M. (2004) 'Buddhist Psychotherapy', www.buddhistpsychotherapy.org.uk/

Short, H. L. (1968) 'From Presbyterian to Unitarian' in C.G. Bolam, J. Goring, *et al.* (eds.) *The English Presbyterians*, London: George Allen and Unwin

Silk, P. A. (2004) 'An interfaith spiritual journey', *Journal of the Unitarian Ministry*, pp23–4

Simons, F. (1983) 'Ministry: the multilingual approach', *Journal of the Unitarian Ministry*, pp21–4

Simons, F. (1985) 'What do we do when we marry?', *Journal of the Unitarian Ministry*, pp.28–32

Smith, M. F. (1996) 'A Personal A to Z of Unitarianism', London: Unitarian Information Department

Smith, M. F. (ed.) (2002) *Prospects for the Unitarian Movement*, London: Lindsey Press

Smith, T. Southwood (1816) *Illustrations of the Divine Government*, London: Lindsey Press

Smith, W. Cantwell (1978) *The Meaning and End of Religion*, London: SPCK

Snelling, J. (1990) *The Elements of Buddhism*, Shaftesbury: Element Books

Sorensen. R. W. (1970) *I Believe in Man*, London: Lindsey Press

Sparham, G. J. (1946) *Khasi Calls: An Adventure in Friendship*, London: Lindsey Press

Spears, R. (1899) 'A memorial sermon', *Christian Life*, 25 March

Spiritualist National Union (2003) 'The Seven Principles', www.snu.org.uk/seven.htm

Starhawk (1979) *Spiral Dance: a Rebirth of the Ancient Religion of the Great Goddess*, San Francisco, USA: Harper Collins

Stringer, A. (2004) 'Quakers and Pendle', www.pendle.net/Attractions/quakers.htm

Tennyson, M. (1992) *Friends and Other Faiths*, London: Quaker Home Service

Thich Nhat Hanh (2003) 'The Fourteen Precepts', www.seaox.com/thich.html

Thomas, J. M. L. (ed.) (1912) *The Order of the Administration of The Lord's Supper*, Birmingham: Thomas Smith & Son

Thomas, R. (1969) 'When is a Unitarian not a Unitarian?' *Transactions of the Unitarian Historical Society*, Vol. XIV, No.3 (October)

Traer, R. (1998) 'The next century', *IARF World*, No. 1, p2

Traer, R. (2000) 'The IARF at 100: looking back and ahead', *IARF World* (December), pp4–7

Travis, C. P. (ed.) (2004) *The Herald* (Journal of the Unitarian Christian Association), Spring

Twinn, K. (ed.) (1959) *Essays in Unitarian Theology*, London: Lindsey Press

Twinn, K. (ed.) (1968) *In Life and Death*, London: Lindsey Press

Tylor, E. B. (1904) *Primitive Culture*, London: John Murray

Union of Liberal and Progressive Synagogues (1967) *Service of the Heart*, London: ULPS

Unitarian Universalist Association (1979) *Hymns for the Celebration of Life*, Boston, USA: UUA

Unitarian Universalist Association (1993) *Singing the Living Tradition*, Boston, USA: Beacon Press

United Lodge of Theosophists (undated-a) *What is Theosophy?*, London: ULT

United Lodge of Theosophists (undated-b) *Letters to an Interested Friend*, London: ULT

Unity of Nations (1967) '"Jesus", now known as 'Sananda', has returned to this Earth', *Voice Universal Newspaper*, June/July/August Issue

Usher, G. (2000) 'Perceptions and potshots: life in the ministerial shooting gallery', *Journal of the Unitarian Ministry*, pp2–7

van der Leeuw, G. (reprint 1948) *Religion in Essence and Manifestation*, Groningen: University of Groningen

van Herwijnen, E. (2000) 'IARF acceptance speech', *IARF World* (April), p2

Walder, R. (2004) 'Unitarianism and world religions – a personal view', *Journal of the Unitarian Ministry*, pp4–5

Weller, P. (2003) 'The dimensions and dynamics of religious discrimination: findings and analysis from the UK', in N. Ghanea (ed.) *The Challenge of Religious Discrimination at the Dawn of the New Millennium*, Leiden: Martinus Nijhoff

Wendte, C. W. (ed.) (1907) *Freedom and Fellowship in Religion: Proceedings and Papers of The Fourth International Congress of Religious Liberals*, Boston, USA: International Council

Werner, K. (1994) *A Popular Dictionary of Hinduism*, Richmond: Curzon Press

Westwood, K. (1998) 'I Will Not Harm the Serpent: Brighid and St. Bride', www.whitedragon.org.uk/articles/brighid.htm

Wigmore-Beddoes, D. G. (ed.) (1975) *Concerning Jesus*, London: Lindsey Press

Wilbur, E. M. (1952) *The History of Unitarianism*, Harvard USA: Harvard University Press

Williams, C. G. (1993) 'The World's Parliament of Religions', *Faith and Freedom*, Volume 46 Part 2, No 137, pp79–94

Wolf, M. L. (reprint 1974) *A Treasury of Kahlil Gibran*, London: Heinemann

Yinger, M. (1970) *The Scientific Study of Religion*, London: Macmillan

Young, M. P. (undated) *Can I Be a Hindu and Unitarian Universalist?*, Boston, USA: Unitarian Universalist Association

Glossary

Advaita Vedanta: a view of reality drawn from the Upanishads that is monistic rather than dualistic (see *monism*).

alchemy: a combination of chemistry and spirituality that seeks a substance known as the 'philosopher's stone' which would change base metals into gold.

apotheosis: deification or deified ideal.

Atman: in Hinduism, the human soul or essential self, identified, in the Upanishads, with Brahman.

Bahá'í religion: a distinct world religion arising out of Shia Islam in the 1860s and founded on the preaching of Baha'u'llah, who taught the oneness of God, the unity of the religions, the harmony of humanity, and the unification of all humanity.

Bhakti: a tradition, within Hinduism, that seeks a close and personal relationship to God.

Brahman: in Hinduism, the eternal, impersonal Absolute Principle.

Dalits: the 'Untouchables', the lowest caste of Hinduism.

Deism: belief in a supreme being who does not intervene in the natural order.

Dhammapada: one of the best-known of the early Buddhist sacred writings.

Dharma: the teaching of the Buddha.

Druze: a religion that arose out of Islam a thousand years ago and survives in the Lebanon, Jordan, and Syria. With some similarities with Islam, it is often referred to as an Islamic sect, but the two differ considerably in belief and practice. The Druze reject polygamy and much of Sharia law, and they teach the transmigration of souls.

expiatory redemption: the belief that the suffering and death of, for example, Jesus Christ, has enabled all humankind to have access to salvation.

Gnosticism: an early Christian 'heresy' which taught that salvation was acquired by knowledge. Some forms of it taught that Jesus Christ only assumed human form and that the crucifixion was a deception intended to fool evil powers.

Haggadah: the liturgical text used by Jews in the order of service for the eve of Passover.

Heilsgeschichte: a form of Christian scholarship arising out of Germany in the nineteenth century that taught that a theologian could find in the fact of his or her own conversion the whole sacred history.

Hermeneutics: the study of texts in order to clarify their meaning for modern readers.

Indology: the study of the history and culture of India.

Irvingites: members of a millennarian Christian sect, founded in the nineteenth century by Charles Irving and now defunct, which was characterised by its vastly elaborate rituals.

Karma: the law that asserts that everyone will experience the effects of their actions.

Karuna: the Buddhist notion of compassion.

Mahayana Buddhism: the form of Buddhism predominant in Tibet, China, Korea, and Japan.

Maronites: members of a major Lebanese Christian Church that has its own form of worship yet acknowledges the authority of the Pope of Rome.

Minjung: the 'oppressed masses' of Korean society.

monism: the belief in the oneness and indivisibility of reality.

monotheism: the belief that only one God exists.

Muggletonians: members of an obscure Christian sect that has long ceased to exist.

Nirvana: the state of enlightenment or of deep inner freedom, the supreme goal of Buddhists.

Nyaya-Vaisheshika: a major theistic philosophical school within Hinduism that uses reason and logic.

Pancha Tantra: one of the ancient scriptures of India.

pantheism: the belief that God equals all creation.

panentheism: the belief that God is in all creation.

phenomenology: a study of religion from 'inside', describing beliefs and practices without external theological suppositions.

philology: the science of language.

Samara: the cycle of birth and rebirth.

Santería: a form of Voodoo found mainly in Cuba, which syncretises the old Yoruba gods of Africa with the Roman Catholic saints.

Shia Islam: the form of Islam observed by the majority of Muslims in Iran and Iraq, characterised by the authority of its clergy and its intense devotional practices.

Shunyata: the notion, in the Kadampa branch of the Buddhist Mahayana tradition, that teaches the emptiness of all things.

syncretism: a mixing of religious beliefs from different traditions.

Taoism: an ancient Chinese religion or philosophy that combines mysticism with science, poetry, and humour.

Theistic Church: a rational religious denomination, now defunct, that existed in Britain in the Victorian period and worshipped God but without any reference to the authority of Jesus.

Theosophy: a religious movement founded by Mrs H. P. Blavatsky, a mixture of Hinduism, Christianity, and Spiritualism.

Theravada Buddhism: the form of Buddhism that predominates in Sri Lanka and South East Asia.

Trimurti: the Hindu trinity of gods, namely Brahma the Creator, Vishnu the Preserver, and Shiva the Destroyer.

Vacanas: free-verse lyrics centering on the Hindu god Shiva, written by four saints of the Bhakti movement.

Vipassana Meditation: a form of meditation within the Buddhist religion.

Voudoun: the form of Voodoo found in Haiti.

Wicca: the form of witchcraft that gathers witches together into covens and practises formalised rituals.

Zend-Avesta: the scripture of the Zoroastrian religion.

Index

Lightning Source UK Ltd.
Milton Keynes UK
UKHW011956170519
342878UK00001B/37/P